Steam from Waterloo

Steam from Waterloo

Colonel H. C. B. Rogers, OBE

DAVID & CHARLES
Newton Abbot   London   North Pomfret (Vt)

British Library Cataloguing in Publication Data

Rogers, H. C. B.
    Steam from Waterloo.
    1. Locomotives – Great Britain – History
    I. Title
    625.2'61'0941   TJ603.4.G7
    ISBN 0-7153-8617-4

Photoset by Typesetters (Birmingham) Ltd,
Smethwick, West Midlands
and printed in Great Britain
by Redwood Burn Ltd., Trowbridge, Wilts
for David & Charles (Publishers) Limited
Brunel House   Newton Abbot   Devon

Published in the United States of America
by David & Charles Inc
North Pomfret   Vermont 05053   USA

Contents

To my wife
who watched King Arthur and his Knights
mirrored in steam

Introduction

If nostalgia is as one dictionary definition has it 'a yearning for the return of past circumstances', then this book is its unashamed advocate. Throughout my conscious life the steam locomotive has been the centre of my enthusiastic interest in railways. In my youth I collected coloured postcards featuring F. Moore's paintings of express trains operated by the old pre-Grouping companies. The focus of attention was always the locomotive at the head of the train, and then in order of importance came the carriages, the railway structures, and the landscape. But the engine was predominant; the rest were ancilliaries. To remove this living creature of steam, smoke, and whirling rods would be analogous to unharnessing the four-horse team from the stagecoach which engine and carriages supplanted. Whatever the brilliance of colour and varnish on the vehicles, glamour and life had gone. Replacement by other forms of railway traction could no more restore the magic than could putting a farm tractor between the shafts of the stagecoach.

Other than one closely-supervised experience at the controls of a 2-8-0 in the Khyber Pass, some half-century ago, I have alas no personal experience of driving and firing. This lack is remedied in the later chapters of this book by the vivid recollections of my friend Mr Jim Marsh, one-time top link fireman on the London & South Western section of British Rail, Southern Region. If this book conveys as he suggests it should the 'smell of steam', then it will be solely due to his own reminiscences – indeed, the book could not have been written without them.

1 Waterloo

This great terminus, which has served most of South Western England since the middle of the nineteenth century, must surely bear one of the proudest names of all the railway stations in the British Isles. Indeed, the only other station in the world which, as far as I can recall, commemorates one of the decisive battles of history is Gare d'Austerlitz in Paris. The name 'Waterloo' is eminently suitable, because most of the historical camps and establishments of the British Army have been and are served by its trains.

The original London terminus of the London & South Western Railway was at Nine Elms, but in 1845 the company obtained powers to move to a more convenient site near the Westminster Bridge Road, close to the south bank of the Thames and with reasonable access to the City and the centres of Government. The ground on which the new station was constructed has been described as being 'formerly occupied by hay-stalls, cow-yards, dung heaps, and similar nuisances.

The move entailed the construction of some 1¾ miles of most expensive railway, for it was carried entirely on brick arches and cast-iron bridges, the latter spanning a number of main streets. The LSWR board had given an undertaking that the extension would be completed by the end of June 1848, a rash promise which caused such a rush over the final stages of the work that its rough finish was rejected by the Board of Trade and the opening was delayed until 11 July.

The first train to enter the new terminus was the up night mail from Southampton on 13 July, arriving at the rather unromantic hour of 4.30am behind J. V. Gooch's new 6ft single express loco-motive *Hornet*. At this time Waterloo was only a small station with three platforms and two middle roads, approached by the four running lines of the extension from Nine Elms. Of these four lines, two were the main lines and the other two were the 'Windsor' lines, which ran to that destination through Staines. These comparatively modest facilities were described by William Chaplin, chairman of the company, as 'amply sufficient for present and future needs'.

At one time it was proposed to extend the railway from Waterloo to the City by a line crossing the Thames near Southwark Bridge. Although the project was not pursued, it did have some influence on a decision to extend one of the middle tracks across what is now the main concourse of the station to join the South Eastern Railway line from London Bridge to Charing Cross by a connection facing London Bridge. This extension was completed in 1864, and here the SER built a station which it named Waterloo Junction.

To meet the various demands to which it was successively sub-jected, Waterloo grew in a rather haphazard way. In 1860 an extension was opened on the north side of the main station, for the Windsor and 'loop line' traffic, which was designated the North Station. In 1878 a South Station was opened. It consisted of a single double-sided platform, forming something of an annexe to the main station, to which it was connected by a covered passageway. Its opening came approximately with the lease by Turkey to Great Britain of the island of Cyprus, so the South Station was inevitably known as 'Cyprus'. In 1885 further platforms were constructed on the north side of the North Station. In that year Khartoum had fallen to the Mahdi and General Gordon had been killed, so that these became 'Khartoum'.

Nomenclature became subsequently somewhat confused, with a South Station, a Central Station, and a North or Windsor Station. The connecting line to the SER became something of a boundary, and notices erected on the removable bridge over that line directed passengers to the South Station on one side and to the North Station on the other. This connecting line was used at one time for LNWR trains between Euston or Willesden Junction and Cannon Street, via Addison Road. The service did not last long, but the connection was in frequent use for the interchange of vehicles between the respective railways and for special trains, including those conveying British and foreign royalty between Windsor and the Channel ports.

The bridge enabled passengers to cross the connecting line behind the buffer stops of Nos 4 and 5 Platforms. It had movable sections which could be drawn back. My earliest memory of all was of crossing that bridge amidst the hiss of steam from London & South Western engines. Looking back, and connecting the episode with family affairs, it must have been when my father's regiment was stationed at Bordon in late 1907 or very early in 1908, after the family had arrived at the South Station; where we went after crossing the bridge I do not recollect, but then I was at the very tender age of only two!

In 1899 and 1900 Parliamentary powers were obtained to reconstruct and enlarge a station which had become very inconvenient in many ways, from the unplanned manner of its expansion. Work started soon after these powers were obtained, but much of it was preparatory and it was not till 1910 that five new platforms on the South side became available for traffic. The Central Station was dealt with next (the connecting line to the SER having been closed), and the completion of the new Waterloo was marked on 21 March 1922 when Queen Mary cut a ribbon to open the Victory Arch.

A fitting reminder that this great station was built by the London & South Western Railway is provided by the magnificent stained-glass window above the main exit from the concourse, which is emblazoned with an achievement of arms of the old Company – the quartered arms of London, Southampton, Salisbury, Winchester, and Portsmouth, within a blue garter inscribed 'London & South Western Railway Company' and

Gradient Profile Waterloo – Salisbury

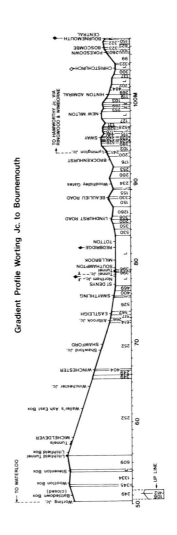

Gradient Profile Worting Jc. to Bournemouth

surmounted by the crest of a dragon's wing. It is unnoticed by the majority of travellers; lacking appropriate lighting, it is too obscure to attract the attention of the hurrying crowds. Our present railway administration often gives the impression of preferring to obliterate any reminders of its precursors.

It is perhaps strange that Waterloo should have been associated so strongly with early electrification, and yet have been the last London terminus into which main line expresses were steam-hauled. Almost until the last days of steam one could look back from the carriage of a train leaving Waterloo and see Drummond's M7 0-4-4 tank engines waiting to pull out empty carriage stock, and so presenting a platform appearance which can have altered little since the last days of the LSWR. Ultimately it was one of the magnificent rebuilt Bulleid Merchant Navy Pacifics, No 35030 *Elder Dempster Lines*, which on Sunday 9 July 1967 worked the last regular steam-hauled express into Waterloo – in fact into London – the 2.11pm from Weymouth. I remember watching one of those locomotives arriving a few days before, and of being somewhat horrified to see the letters SECR on the leading tender axlebox. Not that it was too surprising, because the Ashford axleboxes had been standardised for the Southern Railway, but it would have been nicer to see the letters LSWR.

The main line steam services to and from Waterloo were those connecting it to Southampton, Bournemouth, and Weymouth; to Exeter, Plymouth, and the Atlantic Coast; and to Portsmouth. Other services ran over the long branches to Reading, Guildford, and Winchester via Alton, and the many suburban destinations.

For the first 20 miles out of Waterloo on the main line the gradients are easy. Then at West Byfleet there begins a steady rise for some 11 miles at an average of about 1 in 350 through Woking and Brookwood followed by 12 miles of mostly level line through Farnborough, Fleet, and Winchfield to Hook. The rise resumes through Worting Junction, where the main lines to Bournemouth and the West of England diverge, just over 50 miles from Waterloo. Following the Bournemouth line, the rise

13

continues gently, with one slight fall, to the summit at Litchfield Tunnel at about the 56th milepost. From here the line drops steadily through Micheldever, Winchester and Eastleigh, mostly at 1 in 252, to the 77th milepost. There is then a level stretch of six miles through Southampton. From there on the line is undulating in character through Brockenhurst and Bournemouth, until the sharp 1½-mile rise at 1 in 91 to Bincombe Tunnel, 138 miles from Waterloo, and the subsequent steep fall at 1 in 52, 1 in 60, and 1 in 74 to the terminus at Weymouth.

Considerably more fearsome gradients are encountered on the routes which were pursued by the famous Atlantic Coast Express. From Worting Junction to Andover (66 miles) there is a practically continuous fall, the last three miles of which are 1 in 178. Thence the line rises to beyond the 73rd milepost, the steepest gradient being three miles at 1 in 165; and after this it falls for more than 10 miles to Salisbury (84 miles), including four miles past Porton, at 1 in 140 easing to 1 in 169. From Salisbury there is a steady pull up to Semley (101 miles), and then a steep descent of four miles at 1 in 100, 1 in 114, and 1 in 130 to Gillingham. This is followed by a rise of 2½ miles (including one mile at 1 in 100) to Buckhorn Weston Tunnel, and then a fall of 1 in 100 for two miles and a rise of 1 in 80 for nearly a mile to Templecombe Station. This used to be an important stop, the junction with the Somerset & Dorset Joint Railway, and restarting with a heavy train up the ensuing 1½-mile 1 in 100 gradient could be a problem. Once this gradient is surmounted at the 113½ milepost, there is a steady fall of varying steepness to Yeovil Junction (123 miles), including about 1½ miles at 1 in 80. From Yeovil there is a stiff pull of four miles at from 1 in 140 to 1 in 200, followed by fall to the 130½ milepost, and then three miles at 1 in 80 through Crewkerne to the 133¼ milepost. For the next 13 miles through Axminster the line drops at an average gradient of about 1 in 200. After this comes the hardest climb of all before Exeter – 8½ miles, of which much is at 1 in 70 and 1 in 80. After Honiton Tunnel there is an almost equally difficult bank for up trains of four miles through

Honiton at 1 in 90 to 1 in 100, and then the final 14 miles of steep up and down gradients to Exeter (171¼ miles from Waterloo).

Exeter marked the termination of LSWR really fast running because of the formidable gradients that followed. On the way to Plymouth the line climbs almost continually through Okehampton to the 201st milepost, most of the last 10 miles being at 1 in 77. From this summit thre was a similar fall for 24 miles to the Tavy viaduct, some 10 miles from the terminus at Plymouth Friary. From Coleford Junction on this route, about 12 miles from Exeter, a line branched off to Barnstaple and Ilfracombe. As far as Barnstaple there were fairly easy falling gradients, but the last six miles to Ilfracombe included the terrific climb over the summit at Mortehoe, with gradients rising for 3½ miles, mostly at 1 in 40, and then falling over the last two miles into Ilfracombe at 1 in 36.

The remaining route to be considered, that to Portsmouth, branched south from the main line at Woking. It is by no means an easy route. Just after Milford there is a 1½-mile climb to Whitley at 1 in 82, followed after a short fall by 3½ miles at 1 in 80 to just before Haslemere. From here the line drops for 11 miles, including two miles at 1 in 80 before Liss. After Petersfield there is a fairly steep approach to and beyond Buriton Tunnel, followed by a two-mile descent at in 1 in 80, and then by less severe gradients for some six miles to Havant.

The LSWR was never renowned as a fast railway, and yet in 1847 it came easily next to the Great Western in running the fastest trains in the world, though having far more severe gradients than the latter railway. The Southampton expresses, with two stops, took 1¾ hours over the 77 miles from Nine Elms, and in October 1847 the up trains took 1 hour 40 minutes (46.45mph), as compared with the Great Western timing of 1 hour 37 minutes, with one stop at Didcot, for the 77 miles from Paddington to Swindon (47.66mph).

However, this reputation for high speed did not last long and E. Foxwell, writing in 1889, was somewhat uncomplimentary about the London & South Western and the other railway lines in the south of England, which amalgamated in 1923 to form the Southern Railway. Of the southern lines in general, he wrote:

The traveller who cabs across from Waterloo to Euston, from Victoria to St Pancras, or from London Bridge to King's Cross, is in each case moving to a higher railway atmosphere, where the time-bills are meant to be taken in good faith, where the quality of the service is superb, and where we can rely on its being the rule, not the exception, to carry out what has been contracted for. We say adieu (or *au diable*) to the "cheery stoicism" of that South Western terminus, where in-coming trains arrive at their own sweet time and place, to the subtle irony of the Brighton with its "fast" and very "limited", to the South Eastern with its fore-ordained chronic block in sight of port, to the Chatham with its hand-brakes; and we alight upon platforms of common sense, where efficiency is high, where only fares are low. Good-bye to the sportive tricks of Southern complexity; now we come to stern simplicity, which merely says and does. Only the deeds are first class, though most of the passengers are third.

The Southern lines form a group which must be called a different species if only because they are wanting in that essential characteristic *punctuality* . . . Trains which never (well, hardly ever) throughout the year arrive decently near their time are maddening to everyone except the officials; there is no point in them, they have lost their savour, and are as different from the real article as a stale egg from a fresh one. Besides this lapse in regard to their crowning virtue, there are other reasons why the Southern companies are justly unpopular. They pay very good dividends, yet charge exhorbitant fares . . . But the *South-Western* must be exempted from this particular reproach; it deserves peculiar respect for upholding universal and unconditional third class amid such demoralising companionship though its first and second class fares are high . . .

Where the southern lines, however, most excel the northern ones is in the matter of *Sunday* arrangements. They make the best of this terrible day, not the worst, and deal with conflicting interests in a sensible way . . . The South-Western is very genial, for it starts a "cheap" train at the pleasant hour of half-past nine, and, running at 35 miles an hour inclusive, gives seven hours at Bournemouth before the equally quick return home. On Sunday these four southern companies show in their best colours, and offer a happy contrast to that gloomy dog-in-the-manger policy with which the northern lines disfigure the day.

16

However, treating of these various railways separately, Foxwell obviously rated the London & South Western as considerably better than the others. He said that the LSWR had three reasons for running fast

1. The traffic to Exeter, Plymouth, and the South West generally, was in competition with the GWR. Between London and Exeter the LSWR ran nine fast trains (that is, with an average speed of 35mph or over), while the GWR ran 12. But of the Great Western fast trains, four were restricted to 1st and 2nd class only, whereas the South Western carried 3rd class passengers on all its trains. For tourist traffic to the North Devon resort of Ilfracombe, the LSWR had the advantage because it ran on its own metals the whole way, whereas the GWR carriages were transferred to the LSWR trains at Barnstaple; although the GWR route was shorter by two miles, the LSWR trains took 6½ hours, as compared with the GWR's 7¼ hours,

2. The LSWR took holidaymakers and tourists to Bournemouth, Weymouth, Swanage, and the New Forest. The Bournemouth traffic particularly had been growing rapidly and was so valuable that the company had recently constructed from Brockenhurst a most expensive short cut, giving a saving of eight miles. To Weymouth the LSWR route was 145 miles as against 168 by the GWR, and the former's best trains were 20 minutes quicker than its rival's; the LSWR also gave a better average service.

3. Trains to Portsmouth and Southampton served the pleasure garden of the Isle of Wight, though it was long before there were trains as fast as these services deserved.

Foxwell notes however the LSWR's enormous suburban service, extending to Guildford, Richmond, Windsor, Hampton Court, Leatherhead, Hounslow, Reading, and other destinations. He considers that this swarming traffic had much to do with the rarity of real express trains on its main lines. The 'everlasting stir' at Clapham Junction was notorious.

W. M. Ackworth (later Sir William, KCSI, and described in the *Dictionary of National Biography* as 'the greatest expert in the world on the relationship between railways and governments') presents a different contemporary view of the London & South Western in 1889. He writes:

The South Western Railway forms a fit transition between the great northern and western trunk lines, and what, if one were to insist on an arboreal metaphor, might be called the shrubby lines to the south and east. In one sense, of course, every company has a main line. Even the Metropolitan has one, and it extends from Aldgate to Edgware Road. But the main line of the Brighton Company, for instance, is hidden amidst the labyrinth of branches, many of which start away from the very roots of the central stem, crossing and recrossing and interlacing in almost inextricable confusion; and the mere appearance of the map entirely fails to show that any one road is more important than the rest. Now, if it cannot be said that the original main line from London to Southampton, extended as it has been on to Dorchester and Portland, is an inconspicuous stem, still less that the branch to Exeter, Ilfracombe, Launceston, and Plymouth is anything but a vigorous offshoot; for all that, it is strictly true that the through traffic is by no means so important a part of the South Western business as it is in the case of the northern lines. Compare an express to Birmingham with an express to Portsmouth, the largest town on the South Western system. The Birmingham train drops perhaps half-a-dozen passengers at Northampton and a few more at Coventry, possibly leaves behind at Rugby a carriage for Leamington, but the great bulk of the passengers go through all the way. Suppose, on the other hand, that a train earns an average of £30 on the 74 miles between London and Portsmouth. Not more than £8 or thereabouts of this will be through fares, the rest will be paid by passengers who get in or alight, or both get in and alight, at intermediate stations. . .

A few years back, both in engines and rolling-stock, the South Western had undoubtedly fallen below the mark. The carriages were old and small and inconvenient, and the engines, which had been in the van of progress a generation earlier, were mere pigmies by the side of the giants of the present time.

No traveller on the line can have failed to notice the improvement that has been made recently. New engines of Mr Adams's design, one of which obtained a gold medal at the Newcastle Exhibition of 1887, have been put on by scores, and their immense increase of strength enables the trains to do what they seldom did a year or two back – keep time. So great is the change that has taken place that it is reported that, whereas a short time back on an average 50 per cent of the stock were under repair at any given moment, to-day the proportion has fallen to 30 per cent. The carriages, too, have not been neglected. Though there is still much stock running that could not be described as "replete with every modern convenience", the new carriages on the fast trains to Bournemouth and Exeter leave nothing to be desired. Practically the whole of the stock is fitted with continuous automatic brakes, and a considerable part of it is lighted with gas.

It was after the turn of the century that the London & South Western Railway again became associated with high-speed running. Impetus was given by the races (though they were never officially described as such) between the London & South Western and the Great Western from Plymouth to London. They were occasioned by the calling of the American Line trans-Atlantic steamships at Plymouth, and the subsequent carriage of passengers and mail to London. Until the beginning of the 20th century the Great Western Railway had enjoyed a monopoly of the ocean traffic at Plymouth because of its well-equipped Millbay Docks. Then in 1892 the LSWR was given powers to acquire the almost moribund Southampton Docks as from 1 November of that year, and immediately began their restoration to provide an ocean terminal.

The American Steamship Company (commonly known as the American Line), virtually the only United States company among the North Atlantic passenger shipping lines, traded between New York and Liverpool. It was well aware of the LSWR plans, and in 1892 in conjunction with that company decided to change its British port to Southampton. In September of that year it was announced that the United States Postmaster-General had accepted the tender of the American Steamship Company to carry the American mails from New York to Southampton as from February 1893. The first sailing to Southampton was taken by the *New York* (the former British *City of New York* of the Inman Line) which arrived there on 4 March 1893. In 1895 the American Line had two new 11,629ton ships, the *St Louis* and the *St Paul*, built for the New York–Southampton service. Passengers to and from the European Continent travelled by the LSWR Southampton–Havre service, which connected with the American Line at Southampton. In 1899 the American Line ships began to call at Cherbourg on the way to and from Southampton, to enable them to compete on equal terms with the French and German Trans-Atlantic liners serving French ports. Then came a further step to speed the services to and from England. Outward, instead of running New York–Cherbourg–Southampton, the sailings would be New York–Plymouth–Cherbourg–Southampton, thus saving a day for travellers to London; passengers and mails would be landed at Plymouth by tender. The American Line gave the LSWR plenty of time to make arrangements at Plymouth, and the latter came to an arrangement with the GWR by which the London & South Western would carry the passengers and the Great Western would transport the mails.

At its Stonehouse Pool Quay, the LSWR Western built an excellent passenger terminal, which was connected by a short branch line to its main line a little to the east of Devonport Station, the junction facing towards Plymouth. Because the LSWR line to Exeter ran westwards from Plymouth, boat trains would have to reverse at the junction. The GWR mail trains on the other hand would run directly from Millbay Docks, through Plymouth North Road Station, and thence east towards London.

On the face of it there was no need for competition, but both companies regarded the running of these trains as a matter of prestige. The South Western built new corridor coaches 6in wider than their predecessors for its 'Ocean Specials'. Because the 'Ocean Special' might run at any time of day or night depending on the arrival times of the ships, sleeping cars were also built – the only ones ever to run on the London & South Western. Restaurant cars were included in the trains if their running hours included normal meal times.

The LSWR had far the more difficult route of the two, through the Great Western had eighteen miles further to run because the shortened route via Westbury had not yet been completed and its trains from Exeter were still routed via Bristol. The LSWR had the additional disadvantage of having to cross the Great Western at Exeter. At Cowley Bridge Junction its

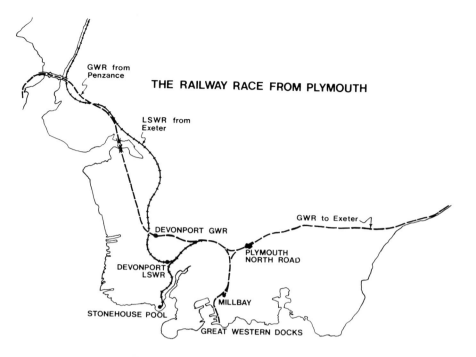

THE RAILWAY RACE FROM PLYMOUTH

GWR from Penzance

LSWR from Exeter

GWR to Exeter

DEVONPORT GWR

PLYMOUTH NORTH ROAD

DEVONPORT LSWR

MILLBAY

STONEHOUSE POOL

GREAT WESTERN DOCKS

trains from Plymouth ran for a mile over the Great Western main line to St David's station at Exeter, travelling on the GWR *down* line (ie in the opposite direction to trains bound for Paddington). From St David's, LSWR trains had to climb a sharply curved gradient of 1 in 37 to reach its own Queen Street (now Central) station at Exeter. Furthermore, the Great Western had the right to hold LSWR trains at St David's.

The new service started with the arrival of the *St Louis* early on 9 April 1904. G. A. Sekon, first editor of *The Railway Magazine*, travelled on the three-coach train and wrote an interesting description of the journey. He says that the 'right away' signal was given at 5.03am and that 'with a passenger tank engine at the head and a four-wheel dock-shunting locomotive at the rear, the special commenced its journey over the stiff and tortuous line some 63 chains in length, which connects the Stonehouse Pool Station with the main line of the London & South Western

Railway a short distance on the Plymouth side of Devonport Station.' They were replaced by Drummond 6ft 1in S11 class No 399, built in 1903 for express services west of Salisbury.

Of the approach to Cowley Junction, Sekon writes: 'Speculation was rife as to whether we should get a clear road . . . Both trains had approached the junction at almost the same time, we having travelled 56 miles 11 chains from Devonport and the Great Western mail special 54 miles 11 chains from Millbay Station.' (The GWR train had left Millbay at 4.59am, so that the LSWR train had made the better timing.) Sekon continued: 'Now we prepared for the expected stop at St David's, hoping . . . that the Great Western Railway would relent and allow us to run through St David's Station. But this was not to be, as the angry and insistent working of our engine whistle informed us: however, the "home" signal was at last lowered, but before us stood, what to a railwayman is an impassable barrier, the platform starting signal at Danger! And so, despite the commanding and continuous screech of our whistle, at danger it remained; we bow to the inevitable and pull up at St David's, the platform Inspector stolidly (yet doubtless satirically) calling out "St. David's, St. David's", as we drew up.'

However, the train was only held for a quarter of a minute, before continuing on its way to Queen Street. In spite of the formidable banks, the 50 miles to Crediton were covered in an hour. Templecombe was reached at 7.43am, and here the stop was made to change engines. No 399 was replaced by Drummond T9 class 4-4-0 No 336 (built in September 1901) which had the larger 6ft 7in coupled wheels considered more appropriate for the easier section east of Salisbury. The arrival at Waterloo was at 9.36am, a very creditable performance. The Great Western train had reached Paddington nineteen minutes earlier, but it consisted of only three vans.

On a subsequent race on 23 April (very appropriately Saint George's Day, for the saint's name had been borne by a very famous LSWR engine of Beattie's design) the London & South Western was clearly the victor. The time to Waterloo was only 4 hours 3 minutes, while the Great Western took 4 hours 12 minutes to Paddington. The LSWR engines were again those that took part in the inaugural run, but it was a heavier train with four corridor bogie coaches, including a dining and kitchen car, weighing altogether 105 tons gross. The run was recorded by that famous railway enthusiast and writer Charles Rous-Marten, who travelled on the LSWR train. It was eclipsed on 9 May by an outstanding Great Western run, also described by Rous-Marten, in which he recorded a speed of over 100mph – the first occasion on which a train was timed at 100mph or over anywhere in the world. The train was carrying the mails from the North German Lloyd liner *Kronprinz Wilhelm*, and the locomotive was No 3440 *City of Truro*, descending Wellington Bank, a four-mile gradient at an average of 1 in 85 from Whiteball Tunnel to Wellington Station in Somerset. The time from Millbay Dock to Paddington was 3 hours 46 minutes. It does not appear that the London & South Western ever attempted to rival this – with the engines available at the time, there was no suitable stretch of line.

Very fast running continued until a most disastrous accident through excessive speed put a stop to all further racing. The accident occurred early on Sunday 1 July 1906. The London & South Western boat express left Devonport at 11.15pm on the Saturday night with about 50 first class passengers, who had landed from the American Line's *New York*. The train consisted of a brake van, three first class 'Eagle' saloon coaches and a kitchen car/brake van, hauled from Devonport to Templecombe by T9 class 4-4-0 No 288. At Templecombe engines were changed, and the T9 was replaced by Drummond L12 class 4-4-0 No 421. Engines of this class were similar to the S11 class but with 6ft 7in coupled wheels. At Salisbury there is a very sharp curve at the eastern end of the station with a heavy speed restriction. The express reached Salisbury at 1.57am, passing the Salisbury West Box at a speed which the horrified signalman reckoned was at least 60mph. A milk empties train was running slowly into the station on an adjacent line; No 421, leaning as it reached the sharp curve, struck the rear of it. It ripped through the milk vans and struck a stationary goods engine, No 421's tender jack-knifing against the cab. The driver and fireman of the express, the guard of the milk train, the fireman of the goods engine, 24 passengers, and a bystander were all killed, and the remaining 26 passengers all suffered some degree of injury. Various reasons for the accident were suggested, but none have ever been proved. When Dugald Drummond examined the engine he found that the regulator was closed but the reversing lever was in practically full forward gear and the vacuum brake handle was in the running position. No 421, was suprisingly little damaged – it was repaired, superheated in 1915, and remained in service until 1951.

In 1949 fireman Jim Marsh was on a L12 when he learned about No 421's accident in rather a strange way. In a letter to the author, he wrote:

> We were stationary in Clapham Yard, Kenny side, when an old chap walked by us. He was obviously an old railwayman and he called out to me, 'What's her number?' The reason for the question was that she had not been in the shops for so long that the gold numbering on the side of her cab had vanished, and on the other side someone had written her number in chalk, '427', I replied. He then got up on the footplate and asked me if I knew the story of her ill-fated sister, No 421. I told him that I had not, and he related how on the 1st July 1906 No 421 had landed up on 'old England' at Salisbury with an up boat train from Plymouth. The way he described the scene (with iron beds, clothing, luggage, strewn all over the roads) made me think that he must have been the driver or perhaps the fireman. It was only later I discovered he could not have been. I never saw him again, but it was certainly a graphic description – may be he was a ghost!'

It would be fitting to close this chapter with a description of the most famous train that ever steamed out of Waterloo – the Atlantic Coast Express – as it appeared in the last issue of the world's most famous timetable, *Bradshaw's Guide* of 1 May to 11 June 1961. The legend in the *Guide* is perhaps the most romantic ever applied to a great railway train: 'ATLANTIC COAST EXPRESS, Restaurant Car Waterloo to Exeter, through carriages to Padstow, Bude, Plymouth, Ilfracombe, Torrington, Exmouth, and Sidmouth.'

The train left Waterloo at 11.00am and the first stop was at Salisbury (83¾ miles from Waterloo) at 12.23pm; the next was Sidmouth Junction (159½ miles) at 1.47pm. There the through carriages for Exmouth and Sidmouth were detached and taken on by the branch train over the 16½ miles to Exmouth, stopping at Ottery St Mary, Tipton St Johns (where the carriage for Sidmouth was detached), Newton Poppleford, East Budleigh, Budleigh Salterton, and Littleham – names which seem almost a poem in themselves. Meanwhile the Atlantic Coast Express had left Sidmouth Junction at 1.49pm and it arrived at Exeter Central at 2.05pm. Here the train was divided. The first portion left Exeter Central at 2.10pm for Ilfracombe and Torrington, reaching Barnstaple Junction at 3.16pm, after stops at Exeter St David's and Eggesford. This portion was again divided; the first part left at 3.18pm, to arrive Ilfracombe at 4.02pm – the second left at 3.23pm, reaching Torrington at 3.54pm. Both parts stopped at all stations.

The second portion of the main train departed from Exeter at 2.20pm, stopping at Exeter St David's and North Tawton before arriving at Okehampton at 3.08pm. This portion was now divided. The first part continued from Okehampton at 3.12pm, reaching Halwill at 3.39pm where there was another division. The first section left at 3.41pm, and stopping at all stations arrived at Padstow, 259¾ miles from Waterloo, at 5.21pm. I have seen the train come slowly and majestically into this picturesque little terminus behind an immaculate rebuilt Drummond T9 4-4-0. It seemed somehow such a fitting engine to bring a part of the Atlantic Coast Express into Waterloo's most distant outpost. The second section left Halwill at 3.45pm and arrived at Bude at 4.21pm.

The second part from Okehampton followed the first at 3.20pm and reached Plymouth (231 miles) at 4.25pm, dropping down along the valley of the Tamar, the traditional boundary between Saxon England and Celtic Cornwall.

25

No other train offered such a variety of destinations that could be reached without change of carriage. Alas, the method of working did not lend itself to main line diesel haulage, supplemented by multiple units on branch lines. The withdrawal of steam was all too soon followed by the closure of the railways over which ran the segments of the Atlantic Coast Express.

2 The Antiques

By the term 'Antiques' I refer to those locomotives designed by Joseph Beattie and his predecessors; certainly the model of a Beattie engine, in all the glory of its chocolate livery, highly polished brass embellishments, and unique lines, would blend far more harmoniously with the contents of a high-quality antique shop than would the products of any other locomotive engineer that I can call to mind. The 2-4-0 express locomotives of Joseph Beattie's later period particularly were beautiful engines, with features which together were peculiar to and characteristic of the London & South Western Railway of the time: outside cylinders, with pronounced overhang in front of the leading carrying wheels, slotted driving wheel splashers, brasscapped chimney, brass manhole cover with Slater spring-balance valves on the centre boiler ring, great slender brass dome on the raised firebox plate, and swept-back top to the driver's spectacle plate.

The first locomotive engineer of the London & South Western was Joseph Woods. He introduced no locomotives of his own design, but like the locomotive engineers of most other railways at this time ordered the most suitable products from the various private manufacturers. He did not stay long with the company, retiring at the end of 1840. He was succeeded by a very different character with a strong personality – John Viret Gooch, brother of Daniel Gooch, who had been appointed locomotive engineer of the neighbouring and rival Great Western Railway some three years earlier.

Unlike his brother Daniel, John Gooch did not like crank

2-4-0 No 71 *Alaric*, with 6ft 6in driving wheels, designed by Joseph Beattie and built in 1893. Note brooms attached to the guard irons, perhaps for snow clearance – see the guard's story in Chapter 2 (*BTC Historical Records*)

axles, and his express engines were 'singles' with outside cylinders. All Daniel's engines had inside cylinders, but they were built to run on the 7ft 0¼in broad gauge, with plenty of room between the frames to accommodate inside cylinders and valve gear. John Gooch ordered many inside-cylinder engines, but this was because needs were urgent and he had to obtain engines from outside contractors while building and organising his own works at Nine Elms.

The first engine built at Nine Elms was a 2-2-2 with 6ft 6in driving wheels and outside cylinders, designed by Gooch and named *Eagle*. It was turned out in November 1843 and was followed by three others of the same class in 1844. The particular interest of these engines was that they had outside cylinders which together with the smokebox were ahead of the leading carrying wheels. This feature was to be characteristic of all future passenger engines designed for the London & South Western Railway, until W. G. Beattie produced his lamentable 4-4-0s of 1877.

Joseph Beattie, who succeeded Gooch in 1850, designed in 1854 a 2-2-2 with 6ft 6in driving wheels, and 12 engines of this type were built between 1855 and 1859. Beattie had doubts as to the suitability of 'singles' for passenger service on the LSWR, so late in 1854 he had a 2-4-0 with 6ft 0in driving wheels built at Nine Elms as an experimental engine, which he named *Titan*. After such teething troubles as uneven tyre wear had been overcome, *Titan* performed so satisfactorily that Beattie had one of his large-wheeled singles, *Ironsides*, reconstructed as a 2-4-0. *Ironsides* met LSWR express passenger needs so much better than in its 2-2-2 form that Beattie never again built an express engine with single driving wheels. The 2-4-0 wheel arrangement became such a favourite with him that 133 were built at Nine Elms to his design for passenger, mixed-traffic, and goods trains. The passenger engines were produced with 6ft 0in driving wheels (39 locomotives), 6ft 6in (61 locomotives) and 7ft 0in (13 locomotives). The last were the first standard gauge coupled engines to have driving wheels of such a large size. The last six of these seven-footers, which came out in 1868, were always stated to be Joseph Beattie's favourite engines. For many years they were stationed at Nine Elms and worked the fastest trains between London and Salisbury. In the later 1870s the earlier engines of this type were replaced on the Salisbury expresses by the 6ft 6in engines and transferred to the London–Southampton service.

The 6ft 0in engines were practically restricted to the

2-4-0 No 99 *Phlegon*, with 7ft driving wheels, built in 1868 and one of a class of 13 locomotives, probably the best known of Beattie's express types

Salisbury–Exeter line, while those of 6ft 6in type worked on all the main line services. They hauled the bulk of the South Western expresses between London and Salisbury, London and Weymouth, as well as many of those on the Salisbury–Exeter section. They also made frequent appearances on the secondary main line from London to Reading.

Beattie, a most ingenious engineer, was noted particularly for his fireboxes and feedwater systems. At this period the almost universal fuel was coke because of the virtual ban on the emission of smoke which could not be avoided when coal was burned in the type of firebox customary at the time. Coke was expensive, and Beattie set about designing a firebox which would burn coal without sending volumes of black smoke from the chimney. After various complex arrangements had been tried and discarded, his final coal-burning firebox comprised front and back chambers, separated by a transverse and inclined water bridge. There were two fireholes, of which the lower was for the back chamber and the upper for the forward chamber. The coal for the forward chamber was thrown over the water bridge and the fire there was kept red-hot and incandescent. Most of the coal was placed in the back chamber, from which the smoke and unburnt gases passed over the bridge and into the front chamber, where combustion was completed by the incandescent fuel.

Like his firebox, Beattie's feedwater heater passed through various evolutionary steps. In its earliest form it looked like a small chimney placed in front of the real one. This was in fact a jet condenser in which some of the exhaust steam was brought into contact with the cold feedwater. In other variations there were instead of the 'baby chimney' two or even three smaller diameter vertical pipes toward the front of the smokebox. The resultant hot water was delivered into a long pipe from which there was a branch, so arranged that when feedwater was required the fireman could turn a cock on the branch pipe, connecting it to a hot water pump to deliver the hot feed into the boiler. When the cock was closed, the hot water passed straight to the tender. A major disadvantage was that oil in the exhaust steam was returned to the boiler, and this was detrimental to the plates. Beattie therefore replaced the jet condenser by an exhaust branch from the blastpipe. This, issuing from the smokebox, was joined by a narrower diameter cold water pipe, fed by a cold water pump, which ran inside the exhaust steampipe, so heating the cold water before it was delivered to the boiler.

At about the same time that Beattie was embodying his economical methods of working in LSWR locomotives, J. Cudworth was doing the same thing to engines of the South Eastern. Each of these eminent engineers had his strong supporters, with the result that a trial between engines fitted with the rival systems was arranged to take place in May and June 1870 on the South Eastern Railway.

Of these trials, and indeed of trials generally between the locomotives of different railways, E. L. Ahrons has written very amusingly (with a great deal of truth) as follows:

> Now it is to some extent an axiom in locomotive circles that when an engine designed and built by Mr L. H. Crosshead, of X Railway, is lent with the consent of the Board for competitive trials against another locomotive designed and constructed by Mr R. H. Crank, of Y Railway, on the road of the latter, Crank's engine almost invariably comes out best. And if it should also come to pass that a return match is played on the metals of X Railway, then Crosshead's engine always plays a very fine innings, being "not out" at the end of it, whilst Crank's engine is either completely stumped or else "improved out". Pursuing the investigation further, three profound conclusions of great scientific value are almost invariably reached as a result of the trials, to wit
>
> 1. that the air of Crank's railway does not agree with Crosshead's engine,
> 2. that on Crosshead's railway the scenery and surroundings do not suit the taste of Crank's locomotive,
> 3. that both engines might just as well have stayed at home.
>
> The trials on Y Railway are carefully conducted by Mr Crank's chief assistant, Mr Biler, who duly sends in a detailed and exhaustive report dealing with the defective points of Crosshead's, and the superlative merits of Crank's engine; whilst Mr Ashpan, outdoor running superintendent of X Railway, compiles a neat little essay on somewhat similar lines, but with the roles of the principal characters

reversed. And, finally, a few years afterwards, when Mr Crank and Mr Crosshead retire for a well earned rest, and Messrs Biler and Ashpan reign in their respective steads, the latter gentlemen promptly scrap most of Crank's apparatus and Crosshead's patent appliances and start on a few little things of their own. Thus the inexorable law of locomotive progress!'

For the contest the LSWR chose two of its latest 2-4-0 engines, built in 1869, No 121 *St George* and No 119 *Vesuvius*. They had 17in by 22in outside cylinders, 6ft 6in coupled wheels, a boiler pressure of 130lb/sq in, a boiler of 3ft 10in diameter, and a grate area of 18sq ft. *St George* was to work both the Dover and the Folkestone expresses on weekdays, and *Vesuvius* (which was also the reserve engine) was to haul them on Sundays. The SER representatives were two of Cudworth's 'Mail' singles, Nos 2 and 27, built in 1865 and 1861 respectively, the former being the crack express engine of the line. They had 17in by 22in inside cylinders, 7ft 0in driving wheels, 130lb/sq in boiler pressure, a boiler diameter of 3ft 10¾in and a grate area of 22.5sq ft. The dimensions of the competing engines were thus very similar; one might have expected that, if the boilers of both classes had been efficiently designed, the larger grate area of the 'Mail' engines would have conferred an advantage.

The South Western engines worked for a month between Cannon Street and the two Channel ports, driven by their own drivers with South Eastern pilotmen. Ahrons says that *St George* 'did not acquit itself at all badly, and even the South Eastern people had to admit that good time was kept, although they claimed the victory for their own engines.' It was recorded officially that *St George* ran the 76 miles from Cannon Street to the Admiralty Pier at Dover in 96 minutes with a train of 14 carriages weighing about 145 tons, an average speed of 45½mph. In fact, both LSWR and SER engines were quite capable of keeping time with trains of this weight, but in fuel economy *St George* showed to advantage over the 'Mail' engine. The latter with 14½ coaches burnt 25½lb/mile, while *St George* with 14 coaches burnt 23¼lb/mile. *Vesuvius*, with a lighter load of 10½ coaches consumed 22lb/mile. As might be expected, the South Eastern authorities were somewhat disgruntled by these figures and their Chairman wrote to his opposite number on the South Western on 12 October 1870 suggesting that the two companies used different methods of calculating their results. The LSWR denied this, and a representative from the Great Eastern Railway was called in to adjudicate. To the disgust of the SER and its partisans he found in favour of Beattie's engines.

Though it was his express 2-4-0 that stole the limelight during Beattie's lifetime, it is by his little 2-4-0 tank engines that he is best remembered now, for three of them were still in service on British Railways until 1962. A total of 85 of these attractive outside-cylinder well tank engines were built between 1863 and 1875, primarily for the London suburban services, and they almost monopolised the short-distance passenger trains out of Waterloo until the arrival of Adams' 4-4-2 tank engines. With their copper-capped chimneys, polished brass domes, and brass splasher bands, the Beattie well tanks must have done much to brighten the Waterloo scene, as they fussed in and out at the head of their salmon-and-brown carriages, or crossed the concourse with exchange vehicles to and from the South Eastern line. They were not confined to the Waterloo services, for many were drafted to country branches. One was shipped to Cornwall in 1893 to work on the Bodmin and Wadebridge line, which was not connected to the remainder of the London & South Western system until 1895. The main line of the Bodmin and Wadebridge Railway, seven miles long, had been opened in 1834, and later that year a 6½-mile branch was completed up the Camel Valley to Wenford Bridge, from which a mineral tramway ran to the De Lanke quarries. Centuries ago these ancient quarries were owned by a direct ancestor of the author, who in 1470 contributed stone from his quarries to the rebuilding of Bodmin Church, which took place between 1469 and 1472. The old church still stands, though as the ruin that it undoubtedly was when the first Beattie tank steamed into Bodmin station. I would like to think that one of them ran along the tramway to the old quarries, but I am

No 329, last of Beattie's famous well-tank engines, built by Beyer Peacock in 1875. It is seen here shunting at Padstow in LSWR days

afraid that it is very unlikely. Still, stone from them presumably was hauled down the Wenford branch.

Doubtless after the unification of the Bodmin and Wadebridge with the main system, more powerful engines found their way to this LSWR Cornish outpost, but right up to the advent of Nationalisation, no other class was found that could equal the performance of the 2-4-0 well tanks on the lightly-laid and sharply curving Wenford Bridge branch.

Dugald Drummond intended to withdraw the three engines which were then working the branch, when in 1900 they were in need of extensive repairs. Nothing else suitable could be found as replacements, and they were accordingly repaired, repainted, and returned. In 1921 they were given brand-new boilers by Urie, and in 1929 they were again in such bad condition that Maunsell ordered complete repair and rebuilding. Finally, at almost the end of the steam era, it was shown that the Great Western 1366 class 0-6-0 pannier tanks could work the Wenford Bridge branch. Historically, there were no more suitable engines in existence, for they were modern descendents – via the 1361 class 0-6-0Ts – of the old Cornwall Minerals Railway tank engines, designed in 1873 specially for the very severe gradients, by F. Trevithick who was the little company's locomotive superintendent. They were built by Sharp Stewart & Co, which delivered 18 of them to the Cornwall Minerals Railway. They had side tanks but no bunkers (a limited supply of coal being carried on top of the tanks) as Trevithick had intended them to work in pairs back-to-back. In a letter to the author, W. N. Pellow (former locomotive running superintendent of the Great Western Railway) wrote:

> I remember the 0-6-0T engines of the Cornwall Mineral Railway, having worked on repairs to quite a few of them in my early days; although by that time the engines had been re-constructed to work as single units. My father remembered them working as pairs with only a limited supply of fuel and one set of footplatemen; but they never made very long journeys in those days. They would haul empty wagons up to the various clay pits and bring down loaded ones to St Blazey yard, where trains of clay were made up for despatch to Par Dock or the port of Fowey. They did the work for which they were designed very well. After some years the engines were fitted with extended frames at the rear, which carried a coal bunker, and also with a covered-in cab, a buffer beam, buffers, and drawgear; so that they were able to work as single units. Some were sent to other parts of the system and worked on dock lines and in other areas where sharp curves existed.

The rebuilding which Pellow mentions was carried out after the Cornwall Minerals Railway was leased to the Great Western in 1877. The GWR purchased nine of the engines, the remaining nine being bought back by Sharp Stewart. Of the latter nine, the Lynn & Fakenham Railway (later part of the Midland & Great Northern Joint) bought eight. The engines acquired by the Great Western proved so useful on the duties mentioned by Pellow, that when they eventually became worn out it was decided to build a modernised version because no other class on the Great Western could undertake their duties. The late H. Holcroft, then in the Swindon drawing office, told me how he was handed a roll of the old drawings and told to get out a completely new set, keeping to the existing patterns and templates, but to bring every detail into line with current Swindon practice. In 1910, therefore, five 0-6-0 outside-cylinder saddle tank engines Nos 1361–5 were turned out from Swindon. In 1934 five more, Nos 1366–71, were built, with pannier tanks instead of saddle tanks. It was these latter engines that replaced the Beattie tanks on the Wenford Bridge branch. It is interesting that the only type of engine found suitable to replace the Beattie tanks in Cornwall was a modification of a contemporary Cornish design.

One could not leave the Beattie era without mentioning his lovely double-framed 0-6-0 goods engines of 1866, although they were not designed by Joseph Beattie, but by the firm that built them, Beyer Peacock & Co. They were so competent that they were regularly rostered in the 1870s for the 11.00pm heavy West of England goods train. In 1875, when a smaller single-framed 0-6-0 goods engine also of Beyer Peacock design was introduced, there was agitation among the enginemen until the newcomers were excluded from working the night West Country, or 'Tavy', goods.

The term 'Tavy' appears in the 1870s, and was most likely applied to the LSWR's first goods services to and from Plymouth. In 1872 a subsidiary of the LSWR reached Lydford, and in accordance with a previous agreement served notice on the broad gauge South Devon Railway to lay mixed-gauge track along its line from Launceston, which from Lydford ran down the valley of the River Tavy to Plymouth – hence the 'Tavy', the original night goods train between Nine Elms and Plymouth. It is possible too that this South Devon branch was known as the Tavy line. Eventually in 1890 the London & South Western opened its own line from Lydford to Plymouth. This also ran down the Tavy valley but entered Plymouth from the west instead of from the east. The name 'Tavy' was still used up till the last years of the steam era as an unofficial name for the down and up night goods trains between Nine Elms and Exeter.

Some idea of the esprit de corps which animated the

South-Western railwaymen of Beattie's time is conveyed by a guard's account of a journey during the great blizzards of the winter of 1880 to 1881. Berkshire, Wiltshire, and Hampshire were particularly hard hit, and the chairman of the Great Western Railway reported that 'We had to excavate 111 miles of snow, varying according to the drift from three feet down to ten feet in depth. We had, unfortunately, fifty-one passenger trains and thirteen goods trains buried in the snow, making a total of sixty-four, and we had blocks on 141 different parts of the system.'

The London & South Western Railway guard gave the following account of his own experience:

'I daresay it was much the same on all the lines. I can only speak for myself, and I know that I never was out in such a storm in all the winters that I've been guard on the London and South Western. Bad enough we had it, in all conscience coming up from Salisbury in the dark night against the east wind, driving and howling incessantly, and the snow enough to blind you if you'd only turn your face straight towards it for a moment; but the truth is you couldn't do it. Yes, I will tell you about it if you think it worth having, at least in my way.

I went down from Waterloo in the morning to bring up a train coming from Exeter on from Salisbury to London. It was blowing wild enough when we started, and the snow whirling round and round us – not in big flakes like you see it fall when in still weather, but in a fine sharp dust, just like glass ground down into powder. Long before we got to our down journey's end the snow had begun to gather deep in the cuttings, the wind sweeping it down from the open country above, and laying it in a sloping bank, running down far across the rails. It is an odd sensation when you are cutting through snow that is not quite enough to stop you, but very near. It is as if you were off the rails, going over stony ground, and something all the time trying hard to shove you back, and then letting you go clean ahead for a minute or two.

But the worst of it hadn't come yet. Our engine made her way through it very fair, and we were not much above half an hour behind when we went into Salisbury station. There we waited for the Exeter train, telegraphed from Gillingham only an hour late. When she came in I took her guard's place, and we started for Waterloo with

nine or ten carriages, and a good many passengers, a little before five
– just after dark, in fact. It has been snowing, snowing, snowing
down there, as elsewhere, all day long; and as we went out of the
lighted station right into the wild open country, I could not help
thinking of what it would be like that night on the great chalk downs,
or on the roads over Salisbury Plain, without a bit of shelter for miles
and miles. Oh, how it did blow! and how the sharp snow-dust came
sweeping down upon us as we went towards it in the teeth of the
wind. We kept on at a good pace, at least on the embankments,
where the line was swept by the gale as clean as twenty thousand
brooms could have made it. On we went till we got into the cuttings
the other side of Andover. There we were again rumbling as if over
stones instead of iron rails, and being shoved back, and then on again
with a start, and then rumbling and bumping, and then on again. I
should think, with you, that the passengers found it unpleasant; but
it was curious how quiet and contented they all seemed. Nobody
cared apparently to peep out even for a moment. The ladies in the
first-class carriages had got foot-warmers, and so had a good many
people in the second- and third-class; but if they wanted anything
more they didn't trouble themselves to make a sign, even when we
stopped a moment at Andover. Somebody, I daresay, had tried to
look out, and finding it took his breath away, and sent the snow
flying in shovelfulls into the carriage, had shut the window quicker
than he opened it. The frost on the panes made it impossible to see
them from the outside, and the lamps inside looked like little tips of
yellow flame upon a tallow candle.

So there they were, all invisible, huddling up together, I daresay,
and longing to hear they were at Woking junction, or somewhere
further still on the way to Waterloo. I knew it would be worse when
we got past Whitchurch, for the deep cuttings are about there; and so
it was. Rumble, rumble, we went again, and again something
shoving us back, and then on, and then back; and then we came to a
dead stand in that comfortless hole, with the snow, that was
continually sweeping down on us, now above the foot-board and even
against the lower part of the carriage doors. I got down with my
lantern, and no sooner did I meet the cutting gale, than my beard and
the lower part of my face was covered over with a thick crust which
you could neither rub nor pull off with the hand. The wind literally
blew me backward, and forced me to keep my chin down on my
chest, and grope along holding by the carriage handles.' [*Here
followed a long dialogue between driver and guard on the best way of
proceeding, which was by uncoupling the train and using the locomotive as
a snowplough*] . . . 'So I did [*unhooked the carriages*] and when Jack

Randall had backed a trifle, or tried to do it, he unhooked, and leaving us behind in that dismal place, whistled and went bang at the snow, and right on, ploughing and cutting into it for three hundred yards or so. Then he backed again, and down we were once more, stoker and all, hooking on and peering with the lantern, and clearing the ash-pan. That is the way we got on; patience it wanted too, with our numb fingers and half-frozen faces.'

And so we leave that devoted trio, struggling through the piled-up snow and bitter weather towards Waterloo, with their picturesque chocolate-and-brass outside-cylinder engine, and its train of 4-wheeled and 6-wheeled salmon-and-brown carriages.

It was the end of an era. Before 1881 was out, Adams' new 4-4-0 express passenger engines would be working the best expresses.

3 William Adams

In 1878 the London & South Western Railway acquired in William Adams one of the most eminent locomotive designers of all time as its mechanical engineer. He first made his mark on the North London Railway, on which he was locomotive superintendent for some 18 years. He designed the first bogie to be provided with lateral traverse for the pivot, and this improved type of bogie was fitted to his inside-cylinder 4-4-0 tank engines of 1865. In 1868 he showed his preference for outside cylinders on engines with a leading bogie by the production of his later and celebrated 4-4-0 tank engines of that year. They became typical of the North London Railway for the remainder of its separate existence.

W. F. Pettigrew became Adams' works manager at Nine Elms and worked very closely with him. He gives the reasons for the introduction by Adams of a range of powerful express passenger engines on the LSWR as follows: 'Owing to the enormous increase in traffic, in the weight and size of modern carriages, the increased weight of trains, and the demand for quicker transit, the older types of South-Western engines became useless.'

Pettigrew is interesting on the primary considerations which governed the design of Adams' engines particularly those intended to work the fast passenger trains. He writes: 'For express work the average speed actually attained is about 45 miles per hour; for goods and local traffic about 30. But such are the exigencies of modern railway requirements that the demand is constantly made for increased speed, and these speeds are kept at the above limits solely owing to the extreme difficulty of designing engines capable of exceeding them when the loads are at all heavy.' Some of this comment is applicable to the present day! Pettigrew amplifies it by saying that based on his own conclusions after many observations and experiments on the London & South Western Railway: 'Well-designed express engines of normal type with driving wheels 7ft in diameter can maintain an *average* speed between stations on the level of 45 miles per hour when the load is heavy and 60 miles per hour when the load is a very light one.' He produces a diagram with graphs, to show that for an engine with driving wheels of 6ft 6in diameter the average speeds would be 42mph and 50mph respectively. This explains the preference of both Adams and Drummond for engines with 6in less diameter for trains west of Salisbury, compared with those working express trains between Waterloo, Salisbury and Bournemouth.

Pettigrew qualifies his argument by showing that his calculations refer to economical working. Thus: 'In calculating the haulage power of locomotive engines, it should be noticed that the loads in general ought to be such as the engine would be able to haul with the maximum of economy – ie with the shortest possible cut-off, viz, 1/5. But if the gradients be short, so that they can be rushed, or if slower speed is allowable on the gradients; or, again, if a longer cut-off may be used and economy sacrificed, then the engines will haul greater loads.'

Pettigrew shows that one of the first things to determine is the size of the cylinders required, in conjunction with a given boiler pressure, to obtain the desired tractive effort. From this it is possible to determine the boiler heating surface necessary. For express engines he cites this as being a minimum of 3.3 times the square of the cylinder diameter, some 1,320sq ft for an engine with cylinders of 20in diameter. But he emphasises that this is a minimum and that, 'For an express engine it is necessary to get as much heating surface as the conditions of the design will allow.

The Adams 4-4-0 express engines for the LSWR were typical

41

of this wheel type designed then and for many years afterwards. They had a deep firebox with level grate, which could be fitted between the coupled axles and which had the advantage of providing a high proportion of heating surface in relation to the grate area. Pettigrew says that traffic managers were always on the lookout for means of reducing the number of trains, in order to lower their departmental expenses, and were continually demanding from locomotive superintendents a locomotive having a power 50% in excess of that developed by existing locomotives. At that time the most powerful locomotive of normal type had 19in by 26in cylinders. To get that 50% extra power, without changing other essentials, would require cylinders with a diameter of 23¼in, and the grate area would have to be increased from the approximately 20sq ft (sufficient for cylinders of the former diameter) to about 30sq ft. But the width of the grate between the frames was limited to 3ft 6in, therefore its length would have to be 8ft 6in. This in turn would entail a distance of 11ft 8in between the centres of the coupled wheels to get a firebox of this length between the coupled axles, and coupling rods of this length were out of the question. This is a most interesting argument because it shows the limitations to the power of steam locomotives in the then existing state of the art. For Adams' express engines were about the most powerful and economical in the country.

Pettigrew cites the conflicting advantages and disadvantages of inside and outside cylinders. They have some bearing, presumably, on the choice which Adams made on his various designs; he always used outside cylinders for his engines with a leading bogie and inside cylinders for those without one.

It would appear that Adams adopted inside cylinders for engines which did not have the steadying effect of a leading bogie and the longer wheel base which it conferred. For instance, the last class of his 4-4-0 express locomotives had about 7ft longer wheelbase than his 0-4-2 mixed-traffic engines. However, Pettigrew himself does not seem to have been convinced as to the superiority of outside cylinders, for when he became locomotive

Adams 460 class 4-4-0 No 474, built in 1884, approaching Earlsfield. With the 7ft 445 class, the 6ft 7in 460s handled most LSWR express services until the early 1890s

superintendent of the Furness Railway he designed a class of express passenger 4-4-0 engines which were very similar to those provided by Adams for the LSWR except that they had inside cylinders. Pettigrew may have thought the Adams engines too rough riding at speed.

Adams took over his duties when the enormous suburban traffic, which had always been a particular feature of the LSWR, was growing rapidly, with consequent increases in the number and weight of the trains provided. The first need was for something more powerful than the little Beattie well tanks to work them. Although these trains were not yet composed of bogie stock, yet the 14 to 16 close-coupled 4-wheeled vehicles of which they normally consisted provided a load too heavy for the Beattie engines to recover any time lost. In 1878 Adams produced a 4-4-0 side and well tank engine, which was soon modified into the 4-4-2 wheel arrangement to permit an increase in coal and water capacity. There followed in 1882 an improved version, known as the Radial Tanks' or 415 class, of which 71 were built up to 1885. These attractive engines had a history somewhat similar to that of the Beattie well tanks which they superseded. Most of them were scrapped in the 1920s, but two were still working on the Lyme Regis branch until October 1928, when both needed heavy repairs. Before this work was undertaken, a South Eastern & Chatham Railway P class 0-6-0 tank engine and one of William Stroudley's celebrated LBSCR D1 class 0-4-2 tank engines were both given trials on the branch. The P class was far too under-powered for the task. The D1 did better – four others of the class were thereupon given cut-down bunkers to lighten their weight and worked the branch trains for some time. However, the severe curves damaged their frames and they also slipped badly in wet weather. So back came the 4-4-2Ts after heavy overhaul and they continued to work the Lyme Regis trains until 1946, when both of them needed repair again. It was apparent that a third engine was necessary and fortunately another of the class was still in existence. It had been sold by the LSWR to the Ministry of Munitions in World War I and subsequently re-sold to the East Kent Railway. There it had been laid aside derelict. The Southern Railway bought it back, gave it a thorough overhaul, and sent it to join the other two on the Lyme Regis branch. In due course the engine from the East Kent became British Railways No 30583, and when it was ultimately withdrawn from service the Bluebell Railway bought it, and some time later sent it to Swindon for a lengthy and heavy repair. The Bluebell Railway painted it at first in the Adams LSWR livery, but it could never have worn that with its Drummond chimney, and it was repainted in Drummond's green with his attractive lining out.

In writing about Adams' engines, Pettigrew was dealing with the period after 1890. In that year the first of the new and improved range of 4-4-0 express locomotives emerged from Nine Elms, and Pettigrew states that they worked the heavy main line express trains over the Bournemouth and West of England main lines. These trains frequently consisted of 19 vehicles, of which four would be bogie carriages weighing 20 tons each, and the total weight behind the tender amounted to some 260 tons. On the Bournemouth line the 12.30pm down express covered the 79¼ miles to Southampton at an average start to stop speed of 47½mph, while the corresponding up train from Bournemouth ran the 78 miles from Southampton to Vauxhall at 50mph. On the Exeter line, the 11.00am from Waterloo (later the Atlantic Coast Express) for Exeter and Plymouth, was booked at 43½mph to Salisbury. In accordance with normal LSWR practice, the first batch of these engines had coupled wheels of 7ft 1in diameter, and were soon followed by others which were nearly identical, but which had 6ft 7in coupled wheels for working on the steep gradients west of Salisbury. The cylinders were 19in by 26in and the boiler pressure, fairly typical for the period, was 175lb/sq in. The cut-off varied from 75% in full gear to the very low figure at that time of 17%.

No 582 of the 7ft 1in class was used for a remarkable series of trials in 1891. These consisted of five runs with trains of different weights from London to Bournemouth, Bournemouth to London, London to Exeter, Exeter to Woking, and London to Salisbury. A striking feature for the time was that the engine was driven with regulator fully open and with a short cut-off. For instance, a cut-off of 17% was recorded at 68mph down a gradient of 1 in 251, at 66mph down 1 in 386, and at 78mph down 1 in 100. Such a method of driving was that advocated by Pettigrew to achieve economical working, and his views were certainly supported by the results. On the first run the coal used per indicated horsepower hour was the amazingly small quantity of 1.98lb. The maximum recorded was 2.38lb on the second run; the others lying between these two figures. No 582 was burning Welsh coal. Although these trials were held in 1891, it was some years before the results were reported to the outside world. An account was eventually given in a paper presented to the Institution of Civil Engineers by W. Adams in collaboration with W. F. Pettigrew.

Since there were no unusual features in the design of these 4-4-0s, the remarkable results achieved must have been due at least partly to Adams' 'Vortex' blastpipe. This ingenious device had an outer annular orifice for steam and an internal circular funnel for the gases; the latter formed the upper portion of a bell-mouthed scoop which was open to and faced the bottom rows of boiler tubes. This arrangement allowed the exhaust steam to be emitted at a lower velocity than with the ordinary blastpipe, and the area of its escape was so proportioned as to reduce to a minimum the back pressure on the pistons. The reduction of the velocity resulted in a more uniform flow of air through the fire, so that no holes were formed in it even if it was thin, and no large cinders were expelled from the chimney, thus allowing spark arrestors to be dispensed with. The eminent French engineer André Chapelon had a very high opinion of this Vortex blastpipe, and he wrote that: 'The fouling of the annular blastpipe seems to have been the sole reason that this excellent arrangement was, rather prematurely moreover, abandoned.'

E. L. Ahrons thought the 6ft 7in engines were even better than their larger wheeled sisters. He says:

> Not only did they seem to run equally as well on the easier eastern section between Waterloo and Salisbury, when they happened to be working expresses over this road, but, according to Mr Rous-Marten, his experiences showed that they attained higher downhill maximum speeds, and, of course, they were better hill-climbers, as would naturally be expected. They were, however, essentially suited to and used for the heavy roads between Salisbury and Exeter, and Exeter and Plymouth, and did very good work on these sections . . . The 8.30am express from Plymouth, at the end of the last century had the fastest booked run on the South Western, viz, Okehampton to Yeoford, 14½ miles in 16 minutes, or 54.4 miles per hour running average, and No 571 on this train, loaded to 125 tons, made the extraordinary timing of 14 min 14 sec, covering several miles at 80 to 82 miles per hour.

These Adams 4-4-0s were remarkably attractive-looking engines and Adams, or the Nine Elms draughtsman responsible for their appearance, was undoubtedly an artist. Part of the distinction of their profile was due to the descending straight line which could be drawn from the top of the tall stovepipe chimney,

Adams A12, or 'Jubilee', class on a passenger train. This engine, No 556, was built in 1893, one of a class numbering 90, which often handled military trains

touching the top of the dome and ending at the rear of the cab roof. When the stovepipe chimney was replaced by one of the Drummond pattern, the effect was lost, yet the Drummond chimney was very pleasing and suited the four-coupled engines far better than their original stovepipes. Pettigrew is interesting on the chimney. He writes: 'The inside diameter of the chimney is a matter of the greatest importance. It is usually made about 2in less than that of the cylinders. Thus, when the diameter of the cylinders is from 17in to 18in, that of the chimney may be 14in at the bottom and 16in at the top . . . The chimney area is sometimes made 12 times that of the blastpipe orifice and $\frac{1}{15}$ of that of the grate area. The length of the chimney is dependent on the diameter of the wheels and size of the boiler . . .' These, then, were the criteria that determined the length of the Adams stovepipe chimney.

The Adams inside-cylinder engines formed a noteworthy group. The first of 70 0-6-0 goods engines was turned out in 1881

Adams 395 class 0-6-0 goods engine, as BR No 30569 (formerly SR No 3163) at Feltham Yard on 8 May 1954. Fifty of them did sterling service overseas in the first world war (*C. R. L. Coles*)

and the last were withdrawn in 1959. These little engines with their 5ft 1in wheels worked the main goods trains and all sorts of other traffic all over the system, including heavy troops trains from and to Bulford, Aldershot, and Okehampton, as well as the race trains and excursion traffic. They were succeeded on most of their mixed-traffic duties by the 0-4-2 Jubilee class (so called because the first came out in 1887, the golden Jubilee of Queen Victoria's accession to the throne) with 6ft 0in coupled wheels. They performed such excellent work that no fewer than 90 were built at Nine Elms and by Neilson & Co. They were perhaps the most generally useful engines that the LSWR ever had. They were seen at the head of many of the army's troop trains, and they worked almost all the race specials to Ascot, Sandown, Kempton Park, Epsom, and Hurst Park. Other common duties included heavy and fast goods trains to the West of England, coal trains between Salisbury and Fremington, excursion traffic to the LSWR's holiday resorts, and ordinary passenger trains between London and Southampton. I saw many of them at Guildford

48

during World War I, and with their Drummond chimneys (which by then they all had), I regarded their frontal view as conforming very closely to that of the Drummond engines with wing plates, which to my youthful eyes was the proper appearance of a London & South Western engine.

To work the heavier suburban services, Adams produced a 0-4-4 side tank version of the Jubilees, with the same cylinders, boilers, and general outline. They were employed on the Reading, Guildford, and other longer-distance suburban trains. A smaller 0-4-4 tank engine was introduced for the inner and lighter suburban traffic. In later years many of these latter were transferred to the Isle of Wight, where resplendent in Southern Railway green and bearing the names of various places on the island they were kept spotlessly clean. At one stage of World War II when we were training for an assault on the Channel Islands (which was cancelled), my duties took me frequently between the Isle of Wight and the mainland. Returning on the paddle steamer from Portsmouth, the sight of these beautiful little engines at the head of the Newport and Ventnor trains at Ryde pier head station was a constant source of delight.

Near the end of his time on the LSWR, Adams built ten 0-6-0 yard shunter tank engines. They were so successful that Adams' successor Dugald Drummond ordered more in successive batches, until they eventually totalled 34. They were very similar to the smaller 0-4-4 tank engines and were a familiar sight at Nine Elms.

4 Dugald Drummond

Dugald Drummond, who succeeded Adams in 1895, had an immense influence on British locomotive design. Apart from his ability as a locomotive engineer, he was one of those towering personalities who have occasionally appeared on the railway scene. Discipline among the footplatemen had slipped somewhat under Adams, and when Drummond took the place of that kindly, popular, and benevolent man, his stern measures to restore discipline and his insistence on the standards that he expected, earned him at first widespread resentment. To many people he appeared irascible and arrogant, and some always disliked him. But many, perhaps most, of the enginemen found themselves (perhaps to their own surprise) acquiring a pride in their chief, together with a pride in their own excellence (which they owed to him) and in the engines with which he provided them. Such was his stature that even in the days of British Railways most drivers and firemen from the South Western section of the Southern Railway, even though they had never served under Drummond, described themselves under the proud title of a 'Drums man' and looked down on footplatemen who came from the South Eastern.

There is an admirable description of Drummond in the obituary which appeared in *The Engineer* of 15 November 1912:

> He was moreover specially endowed with the ability to manage men. There are few others, if any, in this country who understand the management of men as did Dugald Drummond. He always held that the managers should themselves be personally in touch with their

50

workpeople and he rigidly followed this course himself . . . It was undoubtedly the personal interest he took in his men that made Mr Drummond a success in management. He was always approachable, and if severe, always scrupulously just . . . Moreover, the men felt that he was always looking after their interests . . . We must not forget to mention his keen interest in the young men under him. He established classes in the works for their training and wrote, himself, a very admirable little guide to the working of the locomotive for their use.

To the onlooker, Drummond's influence on locomotive design was particularly apparent in the appearance of inside-cylinder 4-4-0 express locomotives on the North British, Caledonian, and London & South Western Railways, to all of which systems he had been locomotive engineer and in that order. Further, his brother Peter produced typical Dugald type 4-4-0s for the Highland Railway and the Glasgow & South Western Railway, on both of which he was successively locomotive superintendent. The Drummond 'trademark' included the wing plates on either side of the smokebox front. All the 4-4-0s designed by him and by his successors on the Scottish railways had them, as did those of his brother Peter. They were not peculiar to Drummond, for Cudworth had used them much earlier on the South Eastern, and James Stirling, having built engines with them on the Glasgow & South Western (where Hugh Smellie continued them), brought them back again to the South Eastern. Some of Craven's London Brighton & South Coast engines had them and Stroudley copied the idea on his LBSCR singles.

The table on the next page lists some of the principal saturated express 4-4-0 classes as they were developed on the NBR, CR, and LSWR, to show the evolution of the typical Drummond design. Principal dimensions are given, but they exclude coupled wheel diameter (because they were all express engines) and also heating surface (because, as André Chapelon maintained, in a well designed boiler the heating surface is of less importance than the size of the grate).

Railway	Year	Class	Designer	Cylinder dimensions in	Boiler diameter ft in	Boiler pressure lb/sq in	Grate area sq ft	Notes
NBR	1877	476	Drummond	18¼ × 26	4 8	175	20	Abbotsford
CR	1884	66	Drummond	18 × 26	4 6¼	150	19.5	
NBR	1894	729	Holmes	18¼ × 26	4 8	175	20.3	
CR	1894	13	Lambie	18 × 26	4 6¼	160	19.5	
CR	1896	721	McIntosh	18¼ × 26	4 9¼		20.63	Dunalastair
CR	1899	900	McIntosh	19 × 26	4 9¼	180	22	
LSWR	1899	T9	Drummond	18½ × 26	4 5	175	24	
NBR	1903	317	Holmes	19 × 26	4 8	190	22.5	
LSWR	1904	L12	Drummond	19 × 26	5 0	175	24	
CR	1904	140	McIntosh	19 × 26	5 0	180	21	
NBR	1909	243	Reid	19 × 26	5 0	190	21.13	Scott
LSWR	1912	D15	Drummond	19½ × 26	5 0	200	27	

One feature apparent from the table opposite is Drummond's insistence on a large grate.

Dugald Drummond's first express locomotives were the 476 or Abbotsford class for the haulage of the through Midland Railway trains from St Pancras over the difficult Waverley route between Carlisle and Edinburgh. From this masterly design all later North British 4-4-0s were developed. They were very large engines for the period and for almost 20 years none significantly bigger were built for any British railway. Their performance, as compared with contemporary designs, was little short of brilliant. As late as 1916 one of them, No 487 *Montrose*, established a notable record in hauling a very light special train from Edinburgh to Carlisle. The 98 miles, including a nine-minute signal stop at Hawick and the steep climbs over the Falahill (9 miles at 1 in 70) and Whitrope (10 miles averaging about 1 in 80) banks, were covered in a total of 104 minutes, or 95 minutes running time. This record stood for the route until it was finally closed.

In 1882, his reputation established, Drummond went to the Caledonian Railway and in his 66 class 4-4-0s of 1884 provided that company with its first modern express locomotives, and set the pattern for engines of that wheel arrangement for the remainder of the Caledonian's separate existence. It is interesting that the 66 class had the bogie designed by Adams, whom Drummond was to succeed on the LSWR. Another Adams' invention that appeared on the Caledonian Railway was his 'Vortex' blastpipe which was fitted to the famous 'single' No 123, designed by Neilson & Co in accordance with Drummond practice. Drummond liked the blastpipe and incorporated it in his small-wheeled 'Coast Bogies' built for the Glasgow–Greenock route. He was sufficiently satisfied with the results obtained to fit it to a new series of his 66 class introduced in 1889. In fact its use was continued on the Caledonian after Drummond's departure, and McIntosh's famous Dunalastairs had it. McIntosh subsequently stopped using it and Drummond abolished it on the LSWR. It is probable that, as Chapelon suggests, the fouling of the annular blastpipe was the reason.

Drummond's first express engine for the LSWR, No 720, was unusual because although there were four driving wheels they were uncoupled, each having a separate pair of cylinders. The idea was probably to dispense with coupling rods so that the axles of the driving wheels could be placed further apart to allow a longer deep firebox to be inserted between them. Although a few more were built, the idea was not pursued and Drummond reverted to coupled engines. It was on No 720 that Drummond introduced the firebox water tubes that he incorporated on most of his subsequent 4-4-0s and 4-6-0s. In his *Lectures on the Working of Locomotive Engines*, he gives the reason for them as follows: 'There are two groups of cross-water tubes in the firebox. These are primarily intended to increase the heating surface from 50 to 100 percent in the firebox, where heating surface is most efficient. They improve the general circulation in the boiler, and particularly the circulation of the water spaces. They also make a very efficient spark arrester.'

In 1899 engines of Drummond's T9 class 4-4-0s started to enter traffic and immediately established an excellent reputation. They were very handsome engines, and when on the Portsmouth expresses in my very youthful days they passed the cricket ground of my prep school, they seemed to epitomise what a South Western engine should look like. Urie started superheating them in 1922 and vastly improved their performance. Their appearance was altered considerably by an extended smokebox and stovepipe chimney, but it still remained very attractive. My last memory of Padstow is of one of them almost striding into the station, with those big coupled wheels, at the head of the Padstow portion of the down Atlantic Coast Express.

In addition to his express engines, Drummond introduced two classes of mixed traffic 4-4-0s in 1901 and 1903, designated K10 and L11 which were nicknamed respectively 'Small Hoppers' and 'Large Hoppers'. They did much useful work but were never superheated.

In 1903 and 1904 Drummond produced larger 4-4-0s of the

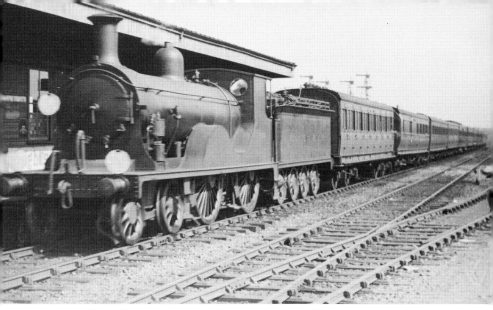

Drummond T9, or 'Greyhound', class 4-4-0 No 338, built in 1901. The engine is in its original non-superheated form. It is approaching Esher with a Bournemouth restaurant car express

S11 and L12 classes. The only major difference between them was that the S11s had coupled wheels of 6ft 1in diameter, while those of the L12s were 6ft 7in. The former (inspired by the success of the 'Large Hoppers' with their 5ft 7in wheels) were intended for the fast trains west of Salisbury, while the L12s were to work the heaviest Bournemouth and West of England expresses east of Salisbury. Both classes proved extremely satisfactory in service. In 1912 there appeared the first of a class which many people regarded as Drummond's *chef d'oeuvre*, the D15 4-4-0 express engines.

Urie started superheating the D15s and L12s in 1915, and the S11s were taken in hand in 1920. With their extended smokeboxes, these engines retained their good looks, but the stovepipe chimneys which some of them acquired later were singularly ugly and I was appalled when I first saw an L12 in this guise at Guildford. A batch of superheated L12s followed Beattie's *St George* to South Eastern metals to meet a requirement for faster running engines than the Wainwright L class!

Drummond L12 class 4-4-0 No 430 at Nine Elms on 16 August 1919. Built in 1905, it is shown as superheated by Urie in 1918

When Maunsell came to Ashford in 1913 from the Great Southern & Western Railway of Ireland, drawings of the design by his predecessor, Wainwright, for a superheated 4-4-0 (the L class) were awaiting despatch to private locomotive building firms. Having no knowledge of the competence of the Ashford drawing office, and preferring to consult his old staff, Maunsell sent the drawings to Joynt, chief draughtsman at Inchicore, asking him to have a look at them and suggest any amendments. Joynt mistakenly advised the reduction of the steam lap to ⁷⁄₈in and a shorter valve travel. Maunsell was as yet unaware of the advantages of long-lap/long-travel valves and accepted this advice. It was a bad mistake. Joynt's practice suited engines having to work the easy schedules of the GS&WR, but it was ruinous to fast running. As H. Holcroft said, in a letter to the author, 'The L class, while being good reliable "old sloggers", would not run at high speed downhill. To get 60mph or more on down grades necessitated full gear and a "breath of steam" in order to get the exhaust steam away.' There was such trouble in keeping time, particularly over the Tonbridge–Ashford section, that in 1925 ten superheated L12s were transferred to the Eastern Section. Here they took over the 80-minute Charing Cross–Dover boat expresses from the L class, and showed themselves to be considerably faster than these latter engines, as well as being most capable. They worked these services until they were replaced by the new L1 class in 1926.

At this stage it would be appropriate to introduce that great steam locomotive enthusiast, Jim Marsh, former top link fireman on the Southern Railway. From a letter to the author are taken some recollections of his early career on the railway

> I started learning to be a fireman in October 1947, just after I was six-teen, and looking back on my early days, I can see how fortunate I was in the various jobs I was given and in the drivers and firemen who taught me. I remember in particular driver Jack Marshall and fireman Bill Plumb. Both of them were so interesting and informative that I used to ask to be put with them, though of course the turns I went on were only 'round the houses', preparing and disposing duties, or else taking empty rolling stock from Waterloo to Clapham. Jack was so keen on rules that he made me learn them parrot fashion. When on a tank engine he would for instance write the Wrong Line Order procedures in chalk on the back of the cab and make me write them down. The next day he would question me on them. On joining the railway we were all issued with a booklet called *Practical Hints for Footplatemen*, and Jack was the model who was photographed to illustrate the actions described in the booklet.
>
> In March 1948 I passed out as a fireman and was graded as a passed cleaner. As such I was give any duty in and around the shed (includ-ing preparing and disposing of engines, and shunting turns), while waiting to be put in the Shed Gang – the first rung on the promotion ladder.
>
> Most of the jobs given to passed cleaners in those days were spare duties in the very early mornings. Around 2.00am or 3.00am there was always someone late or sick. I recall one morning when I was 'spare' and the fireman did not turn up to work the Woking Fish. I had been on a couple of hours and was the only spare fireman in the Loco. We always had for this turn either a Drummond 'Hopper' (L11 class) or his 'Black Motor' (700 class) 0-6-0. I got on the foot-plate and started getting her ready. The driver asked the obvious question. 'How many firing turns have you got?' I replied, 'A

Driver George Newton in the cab of Drummond M7 class 0-4-4 tank No 30132 at Clapham Junction waiting to take empty stock to Waterloo in 1949 (*J. Marsh*)

couple'. He turned immediately to the foreman and said, 'I want a fireman'. He was soon told that it was either me or no one. Indeed, this early turn was so unpopular that I have known drivers and fireman come in late on purpose to miss it. Anyway, we made our way down to Clapham to pick up our fish train, which was fully-fitted and was limited to some 28 to 35 vans. Fish can be very heavy and this train had almost express timing. If I remember rightly, we had a 'Hopper'. The driver, not being very experienced and having no confidence in me, started ordering me to do this and do that. Now an immature fireman can be expected to be told what to do, but to be continually nagged can only impair his firing.

The Farnborough paper train was a similar turn, and for this we used to have a Drummond L12 or, if one was really lucky, a Drummond D15. This train also ran to an express timing to Woking, but then crawling to Brookwood and Farnborough. On this I encountered a 'do this, do that' driver, and again we were 'down and out' – mostly due to my inexperience, but partly the fault of the driver.

After about three months of this, without going any further than Farnborough, but acquiring considerable expertise in preparing and disposing of engines, I eventually got put in the Shed Gang – at last the next rung in promotion, but I was only there for six weeks. We were losing firemen temporarily for National Service at the rate of six to eight a week, and in consequence I got another step up the ladder to the Hopper Gang and, after a further six weeks I went over to the Yard Gang and a little Adams G6 0-6-0 shunter tank.

I was Bert Hooker's fireman over the Yard. He was very keen and conscientious and his engine was spotless. In 1948 he was one of the two lucky fireman to take part in the Locomotive Exchanges, and I remember him telling me some delightful stories. It was with him that I first really started learning how to fire to an engine and to have a clean footplate. After six delightful weeks with Bert, I moved again – to the Clapham Shunter Gang. In those days we had a Wainwright SECR engine with little doors on the sides. The driver I had there was the only one I was with that I did not like. He came to Nine Elms on promotion to driver and had not been driving very long. Furthermore, he came from Feltham, and the Nine Elms men had no very high opinion of that shed's drivers and firemen.

In the first week of January 1949 I went into the Tank Gang. My driver, George Newton, was a *master* tank engineman. We had our own engine, a Drummond M7 motor tank, No 30132 – a little beauty. When we started work on that first morning, my driver said, 'If ever you come on duty and she is in the shed and not allocated to

Fireman Jim Marsh (left) and Driver Tom Smaldon with rebuilt Merchant Navy Pacific No 35018 *British India Line* at Branksome after working the Bournemouth Belle from Waterloo in May 1956 (Courtesy *J. Marsh*)

us, do not get on any other engine – she is ours, unless of course she is on shed washout.' During those delightful 10 months he taught me how to fire to a tank engine, and also a few tricks of the trade. In all this time she was never out of service, other than washout every few weeks or so.

Prior to the 1951 Festival of Britain Exhibition on the South Bank, we always used black hard coal. I cannot say that it was Yorkshire Hard, because we were not allocated the best coal. Occasionally, however, we did get Yorkshire Hard – a long knob of black shiny coal with a thin gold line running through it. When you hit it with a coal pick there was a ring to it and a jarring effect. Because hard coal usually produced more smoke than soft coal, we were in 1950 given

Welsh coal. With hard coal on No 132, I used to leave Clapham with only three to four inches of red hot fire all over the box, even on our heaviest train, the Bournemouth Belle which with its 12 Pullmans and a van weighed 520 tons. On the way to Waterloo, George used to hold a cloth in front of the fire, and if it was sucked towards the fire too quickly he would ease the regulator. I have seen other drivers do this on a 'big 'un', but never on a tank engine. Working with him, I would very occasionally have to put a couple over the half door on the way to Waterloo, and I used to run her into the station with the fire actually out in places to keep her quiet. To do the same job with other drivers, I needed a box of fire.

I recall another nice old tank driver, Sam Mathews, and his fireman, Arthur Smith. Their engine was M7 No 30123. They had fitted lino on their boxes and seats to keep their clothes clean, and around the bottom of the boiler Sam had fixed polished pieces of metal to keep the dust down and the draught out.

On reflection, some of the things that these old boys got up were strange. For instance, if we were in Waterloo in the morning, I was always sent back to get a couple of papers that the commuters had left in the carriages, and George always called out, 'Don't forget *The Times*'. It was considered the best paper for cleaning the windows.

On leaving the Loco, the last thing I would do after taking coal and cleaning the roof would be to pop round to the firelighters and get a couple of buckets of grit that had been sifted from the sandhoppers. Nine Elms was in a dip, and when leaving the Loco there was quite a steep incline to get up. George would deliberately make the locomotive 'dance', while at the same time he would take hold of the firebox door handle (which was on his side) and open and close the firebox door as we were climbing and slipping. I would put this grit up onto the tube plate and you could hear the grit whistle through the tubes and see the muck come out of the chimney. No wonder she always steamed well. He was the only driver who showed me this, and I used to do it on practically every other engine on leaving the Loco, and sometimes I kept a bucket or two for other banks. Strangely, I never saw any other fireman doing the same thing.

One afternoon, when we were in Wimbldon or Surbiton yard, I heard George say rather gleefully, 'I spy axle boxes'. I had no idea what he was talking about, but he pointed out a couple of old wagons that had grease axleboxes (which were fast disappearing). 'Get me a handful', he said. I thought at first he was joking, but he wasn't, so I went and got a handful of grease. We then went round to the front of the engine. After closing the firebox doors, he opened the smokebox door, and, taking the grease, poured a quantity of thick vacuum oil on it. 'Get up in the cab', he said. 'put the handbrake on, the lever in the middle, and open the regulator very gradually.' He then dropped this mess down the blastpipe. 'Do her the world of good', he chortled. In fact most tank drivers did that to their engines. I recall on one occasion a driver in the canteen telling a story of how he was doing this to this engine, when the fireman opened the regulator too quickly and the whole sticky mess was shot high in the air.

If engines were not steaming properly, some drivers would 'cut their throats'. They would get a bucket handle and fix it across the top of the blastpipe. You could not do this to a Bullied for it would make it 'cough'; furthermore, if it was not done properly it could make matters worse, so that the engine would go right off the boil, especially if the blow ring was obstructed. What characters these old drivers were! They really loved their engines.

At the end of September 1949 George retired. We started work that morning at 2.00am and finished work at Vauxhall at 10.00am. We walked down to the Loco for the last time together. In his pay packet there was a slip of paper which read, 'Driver G. Newton, this is to inform you that to-day is the last day of your service.' No gold watches in those days, no pensions, no brass bands. I never saw him again.

Marsh, who finished his time on the railway in 1956 as a top link fireman, knew all the Drummond express 4-4-0s. The S11s and L12s were known to the enginemen as 'Slide Valve Bulldogs', whilst the D15s were 'Piston Valve Bulldogs'. Marsh thought that the latter were similar in many respects to their big sisters, the 'Paddleboats', the T14 4-6-0s, having the same high arched cabs, shaped windows, and little steps on the footplate. In his opinion they were 'the most beautiful of all the old-fashioned type engines.' In a letter to the author, Marsh recalls firing the D15s on many occasions in the summers of from 1952 to 1955, when he was in the No 2 Link (more affectionately known as the 'Hungry 48') when his driver was Fred Whatley. They used to have them on Saturday mornings in the summer months on non-stop specials to Brockenhurst. He last fired on in the summer of 1955, after which he fired to Tom Snealdon in the top link.

In *Lectures on the Working of Locomotives*, Drummond includes in his duties of a fireman to: 'Learn the art of firing properly so that he may take all the possible heat out of the coal used for maintaining a full head of steam, short of blowing off through the safety valves . . . Air is the essential agent in producing combustion . . . It is therefore of first importance to firemen to know how to control it efficiently . . . The centre of the fire should be just as deep but no deeper than is necessary to prevent more air passing through the fire than is necessary for the proper combustion of the fuel . . . The boiler must be supplied with an almost constant supply of water, and never more than two-thirds up the gauge glass, so as to ensure that the engine will be supplied with dry steam at a constant pressure and so enable the driver to work at the highest degree of expansion.'

Marsh was not so keen on the T9 class 4-4-0s. He wrote:

The T9s, or 'Greyhounds' as the old timers called them, were pretty looking engines, especially the always well turned out No 119 in her green livery, but in my view they looked delicate; compared with the height of 'Paddleboats' and piston-valve 'Bulldogs', they were so low that their fireboxes were almost on the floor. And they could not match the 'Bulldogs' for beauty. I have often fired T9s; we used to have turns to Guildford and Teddington with them. I remember one summer Sunday morning with No 119, before I went into the Army in 1949. We had empty stock from Guildford to Waterloo, and I was firing lightly but frequently over the half door. The driver I had was not my regular one and he kept telling me to take a rest. As it was an ordinary stock train with no special timings we were plodding along quite well, but he became so insistent that I should sit down that eventually I did. Consequently she started to fall back, and we started to lose water for steam. We arrived at Waterloo almost 'down and out', and when we were stopped for signals at Westminster Bridge, I had to work like mad to get her going. The driver was obviously not used to the way I was firing – only half shovel fulls at a time – and was under the impression that I had a box full. He got a shock when he looked inside and saw the fire nearly out. I think he had felt he was making me work too hard (which was not the case). Apart from this incident, I never saw any of these engines really taxed or worked hard, or, indeed, put under any pressure.

No 119 had been the Royal engine before the start of World War II, and hence her immaculate livery. Sister engine No 120 has been preserved and at the time of writing is on loan from the

National Railway Museum to the Mid-Hants Railway, where it has been restored to working order as BR 30120.

Marsh's connection with L12 class No 427 has already been mentioned. He says that he often had L12s on Teddington, Guildford, and parcels trains, but that these 'Slide Valve Bulldogs' could not match the piston valve D15s. However, he never saw an L12 really taxed and cannot recall having been in difficulties with one.

One of Drummond's most successful designs was his M7 class of 0-4-4 tank engines. Like the 4-4-0 tender engines, they were developments of tank locomotives built for other railways. Their origin lay in Stroudley's 0-4-2 tank engines built for the London Brighton & South Coast Railway when Drummond was works manager at Brighton. These delightful little engines could be seen all over the LBSCR system. I remember them well when they had the monopoly of the Horsham to Guildford line in the latter period of World War I. I used to cycle to Cranleigh station to watch a spotlessly clean brown-liveried D Tank bring in a morning train from Horsham over the level crossing.

When he moved to the North British Railway, Drummond produced a larger version of the type, which was later altered to a 0-4-4 wheel arrangement because of the weight at the rear end. He built some more very like the North British Engines for the Caledonian Railway, and those for the LSWR were a further development.

The LSWR M7s were most attractive little engines in appearance and excellent in their performance. They were very much part of the Waterloo scene until the last day of steam. I remember the appearance of some Great Western pannier tank engines at Waterloo on transfer and the antagonism with which they were greeted by the Southern enginemen. I asked the driver of a M7 what he thought of them. He snorted indignantly and replied: 'They're not a patch on our engines!'

One last class of Drummond's deserves mention – a class which resulted from a requirement agreed during Adams' time for more 0-6-0 goods engines, but which were never designed owing to the deterioration to his health. Drummond met this requirement by designing a modified version of a class of 0-6-0s which he had produced for the Caledonian Railway. The very successful LSWR engines never received the usual letter and number designations but were always known as the 700 class and acquired the nickname 'Black Motors'.

5 Dugald Drummond's 4-6-0s

Drummond's 4-6-0s have had on the whole a bad press, but for many people they had a fascination and an individuality which to merit treatment in a separate chapter. Admittedly, when I fell in love with them, I was a very young and very ignorant enthusiast, and it was their magnificent appearance that so impressed me; about their ability I knew nothing. The first series were hardly fliers, but the second lot did much good work, and the superheated Paddleboats were the LSWR's best and fastest heavy express engines until the metamorphosis of Urie's shy-steaming N15s into Maunsell's brilliant King Arthurs.

The 330, or F13, class of 1905 were intended to work passenger trains over the heavy gradients of the Salisbury–Exeter line, but they turned out to be remarkably sluggish and were soon relegated to heavy goods trains. An improved version, the solitary E14 class No 335, was no better.

The G14s of 1908 and the similar, but slightly modified, P14s of 1910–11 were much more successful, and from the time of their introduction they had almost a monopoly of the heavier express trains west of Salisbury. The first one I ever saw was in 1916 or 1917, entering Guildford on a down Portsmouth and Isle of Wight express, which we were waiting to board. We then lived at Cranleigh, and for the first time I saw a London & South Western engine which looked more imposing than the brown Atlantics which hauled our train, after travelling to Horsham to join an LBSCR express for our Isle of Wight holiday. To my eyes it was magnificent, looking just what I expected of a big LSWR

Dugald Drummond (second from left) inspecting P14 class 4-6-0 No 448 at Eastleigh in October 1910, where the engine had just been completed

engine, smokebox wing plates and all!

It was not long before my affections were seduced by the T14s, or 'Paddleboats'. Their lovely lines and impressive grandeur have rarely in my opinion been equalled. I saw one first at Waterloo at the head of the LSWR's familiar salmon-and-brown coaches forming a down Bournemouth express. With their 6ft 7in coupled wheels (as compared with the 6ft 1in of the G14s) they were intended for the Waterloo–Salisbury and Waterloo–Bournemouth expresses. As rebuilt by Urie with a superheater and extended smokebox, their good looks remained unimpaired. A later rebuilding by Maunsell with the deep splashers replaced by raised running plates spoiled their appearance, and the horrible little stovepipe chimneys of 1940 would have aroused Drummond's terrible wrath.

Cecil J. Allen had a run behind one of the T14 class which he described in *The Railway Magazine* in 1912 as 'a run of really wonderful merit'. Urie's superheating vastly improved them, and whilst his N15s were having trouble with their steaming, the

67

T14s were the only LSWR engines capable of reliable timekeeping with heavy express passenger trains.

Before World War II, I saw a delightful model of an 00 gauge superheated T14 in the window of Messrs Walker & Holzapfel's shop in the Marylebone Road. It was priced at £20, which in 1939 was quite beyond the pocket of an impecunious army captain with a wife and two children. I went back on my return from Middle East in 1947, but Walker & Holzapfel, alas, had gone.

Fireman Marsh has his memories of the Paddleboats or, as he says some of the old timers called them, the 'Big Drums'. He writes:

> I remember the first time I ever saw a Paddleboat (it was 444) and one of the cleaners said, 'What a good brag hand.' Although I started work on the railway in 1945, I was not permitted to work in the Loco until I was 16, and that was in 1947. I had been working in the Loco for about a week when I saw this Paddleboat. In the half light she looked enormous. She was standing all quiet and her short 'chummy' disappeared into the roof vents. On reflection, I think she looked so large because she was painted black and had no nameplates or windshields to 'break her down'. Standing beside her I felt like a

Drummond T14, or 'Paddleboat', class 4-6-0 No 447 at Nine Elms on 18 October 1913. The engine is shown in its original non-superheated form

T14 class No 458, superheated by Urie in April 1914, and with the large splashers removed and the running plate raised over the coupled wheels by Maunsell

midget, and I am 6ft 2in. I know for example that Nelsons are longer, but they never looked so long as this breed. Eventually we finished cleaning and I stood back to look at her. She was beautiful! I clambered up on to the footplate and in the dark fell over lumps of coal and wood left on the floor by the fire-lighters. I discovered that because she was so tall, with her high-arched cab, there were little wooden steps or boxes to stand on to reach the main steam valve, and when one fired to her one stood in the well. With her 5,800-galon tender, she really was massive.

When I came out of the Army in 1951, I remember asking a friend where the Paddleboats had gone. I suppose I must have been rather naïve because I was more than surprised when he replied in such a matter of fact way, 'scrapped'. It was the first time I realised that they scrapped locomotives! I thought they went on for ever. It seemed strange to me that in the 1950s we were still using Stirling's O class 0-6-0 tender engines (which were sometimes called the 'Flying Bedsteads') built in the 1890s, whilst here were engines built some 15 to 20 years later being scrapped. My beautiful dinosaurs had gone!

6 Robert Urie

Urie, who succeeded Drummond, initiated a type of locomotive that eventually became standardised in the various engines designed by R. A. Riddles for British Railways: a type which to provide easy access to the working parts had two outside cylinders, outside Walschaert valve gear, and high running plates which totally exposed the coupled wheels.

The first Urie engines were ten mixed-traffic 4-6-0s with 6ft 0in coupled wheels, turned out in 1914. Though they did not look like London & South Western engines to me, I so admired their appearance that many years later I built a wood and cardboard model. It vanished, alas, with much else during World War II. These mixed-traffic engines were designed Class H15 and were intended for all kinds of general duty work, from heavy goods to passenger trains, but a poorly designed steam circuit precluded really fast running. After comparative trials with saturated and superheated steam, all of them were superheated.

In 1914 Drummond's E14 4-6-0 No 335 was rebuilt as an H15, retaining its old boiler shell and flat grate, compared with the sloping grates of the H15s proper. All these engines did excellent work during World War I, and ten more were ordered by the LSWR, although work on them did not start until after the Grouping of 1923 which produced the Southern Railway. These differed from the original engines of the class in having stovepipe chimneys instead of the Drummond pattern, and coned instead of parallel boiler barrels. There were other minor modifications. These ten later H15s entered traffic in 1925. Urie had also intended to convert Drummond's five F13 class 4-6-0s into H15s, and they too were so rebuilt in 1924; thus by the beginning of 1925 the class consisted of 26 engines.

Of the H15s, fireman Jim Marsh writes:

They were nice engines, and provided they had a clean fire nearly always steamed and behaved well. We used to have them on stopping trains to Basingstoke and Salisbury and often on freight trains. I well remember having one of the '490 breed' (as we often called them) in the winter of 1952–53 on the 12.45am Nine Elms goods to Basingstoke. I was with driver Joe McCarthy, who had very bushy eyebrows and a moustache, and used to wear a civvy cap back to front driving. It was a freezing cold night and we were both wearing our overcoats. I left the firebox doors fully open and fired to her nice and steady. It was not a quick train but I was kept very busy, especially when we got out of London, because it got colder and every couple of minutes or so I had to alternate the injectors in case they froze up. Approaching Esher, Joe came inside for a cup of tea, and I noticed that his eyebrows and moustache were covered in frost. I put the 'pep' pipe onto the coal in the tender to keep the dust down, and some of the hot water went on to the shovel plate and shovel. When I looked round a couple of minutes later I was surprised to see ice on them, and this on a steam engine with the firebox doors wide open! Fortunately she steamed well and we had a good trip. We came off at Basingstoke and took her into the Loco to work the up 6.30am "stopper" to Waterloo. However, while in the depot I had to keep popping out of the cabin to the engine to alternate the injectors so that they would not freeze up. I remember that they had put very large oil drums full of red hot coals and wood all round the depot to keep the engines warm.

Marsh relates a curious incident in which the very first of the H15s, No 486 (by then No 30486) figured – an incident which he considered exposed the fallacy that 'working to rule' (ie following the instructions laid down in the rule book) meant observing out-of-date practices. Marsh left the Army in 1951 at the end of his National Service, and on returning to the railway found that during his absence he had been promoted several times. When he had been called up he was in the 'Tank Gang', but had passed through many of the lower links during his service and was now in the 'Feltham Gang' with a driver named Jack de Barr. Marsh writes of the incident as follows:

It was in the winter of 1951. We had worked to Feltham and were then booked to work the midnight coal train to Surbiton and Nine Elms. We had No 30486, a H15 class 4-6-0, and the guard came up to say that we had 'equal to 90' (loose-fitted coal wagons). On arrival at [Virginia Water] we had a full head of steam and half a glass of water. Descending towards Chertsey with these loose-coupled wagons, the guard, as he came over the top, carried out his duty of putting on his handbrake to keep the couplings taut. We had passed Chertsey and had started the climb towards Addlestone Junction and the main line at Weybridge, when Jack called out, 'They are pulling a bit heavy'. [The guard had in fact dropped off to sleep, leaving his brake on] As per rule book I went to the signalman at Weybridge, crossing the main line (which is not very nice in the dark, especially with so many electric lines) and told him that we had come to rest just a few feet inside his home signal and what train we were. He replied, 'Fine; as you are inside my home signal you do not need any wrong line order forms. I want you to part your train, take the first 25 into Weybridge yard and leave them, then go back on the wrong road, collect the rest of your train and take them on to London.' I thought that this was good – no shunting at Surbiton, but straight on to London, so that we would finish early. I went back to the footplate and told my mate what we were to do, and then changed the headcode from the front of the engine to the back. The shunter came up and parted half the train, after which we pulled into Weybridge yard, unhooked, and waited for the signalman to tell us to proceed back on the wrong line to the rear half of our train.

After we had been waiting for some 20 minutes with no sign of activity, Jack said he would go across and see the signalman. It was another 20 minutes before he came back. He told me that when the shunter had parted our train he had failed to pin down any brakes on the remaining wagons and as we moved off the rumbling had set the other half racing back down the bank on the wrong road towards Addlestone. I now had to carry out the Wrong Line procedure.

I went over to the signalman at Weybridge and he handed me his yellow Wrong Line order form, on which it was stated that he would not move any traffic in his area until I returned it to him

Urie N15 class 4-6-0 No 737 (later named *King Uther*) hauling an express for Exeter. This locomotive was built in 1918

countersigned by the signalman at Addlestone Junction. When I got there the signalman told me that he had heard me coming and falling over his signal wires. He was very pale, and told me that after our train had passed he was just going to have a cup of tea when, hearing a whistle blowing, he looked out and saw the runaway coal wagons careering down the bank. At the bottom there was another coal train which had been behind us and the wagons were closing fast. He had the presence of mind to throw the road over, so that the wagons were switched to the right road. How they stood up he did not know. He said that he had never seen an electric train come down that stretch as fast as those coal wagons.

I returned to Weybridge with the yellow form duly counter-signed and got permission to start off and collect the rear of our train. I spoke to poor old Joe, who was like a ghost. He had been standing at the rear of his van blowing his whistle for dear life, while looking at the stationary goods train and expecting to be killed.

A few weeks later an enquiry was held at Weybridge station. The shunter was reprimanded because as he had parted the train it was his duty to pin down the brakes. Had I done so, it would have been my responsibility. The guard was suspended for three days and the signalman at Addlestone was commended for averting a near disaster.

This is a most interesting record of the Rule Book in action, showing the relationship between footplatemen and signalmen, the authority vested in the latter, and the duties of firemen in occurrences of this nature.

In August 1918 Urie produced the first of his 4-6-0 express passenger locomotives, No 736. In general design it was very similar to his H15s, except for the larger driving wheels, slightly tapered boiler, and stovepipe chimney. Ten of this N15 class were turned out in 1918–19 and a further ten in 1922–23. As originally built they were not an entire success. Like all Urie engines they were massively constructed, of simple straightforward design, and with ample bearing surfaces. Their running suffered from a poor steam circuit, and steam pressure could not be reliably maintained. They were not effective replacements for the Drummond engines on the heavier express trains. When Maunsell became chief mechanical engineer of the newly-formed Southern Railway, he took this steaming trouble in hand. After much experiment the trouble was eventually cured by replacing the Urie stovepipe by the Drummond chimney fitted to the H15s, with the addition of a capuchon and other minor alterations. This, with its larger petticoat pipe, allowed the blastpipe cap to be enlarged from 5in to 5⅛in. Maximum indicated horsepower now rose from the original 950 to 1,250. Similar modifications were made to the other 19 engines, and this type of chimney became standard for the later King Arthur, Schools, and Lord Nelson classes.

When the later Maunsell-designed N15s were given the names of the Knights of the Round Table, the Urie N15s were given other names associated with the King Arthur legends. The last of the class (and the last London & South Western engine) was No 755 *The Red Knight*. This engine seems to have had special

Urie Class N15 4-6-0 No 740 in original condition

treatment at Nine Elms shed; Marsh says that he was told by many people who worked there during World War II that if there were only two clean engines in the shed or on the railway one would be No 755 and the other the T9 class 'Royal' engine No 119. On No 119 the inside motion was painted red, the rest of the engine was box-panelled (including the wheels), and the brass hooter was highly polished.

The crack goods train on the LSWR, certainly from the 1870s, was the fast night goods between London and Plymouth, known as the 'Tavy', as related in Chapter 2. In the early 1950s Marsh was in the 'Tavy gang' which worked this train and he had a curious experience on it. He writes:

We used to sign on at 8.14 pm at Vauxhall and work a stopping train – the 8.54pm, all stations after Woking to Salisbury. On this particular night in 1953 I was with Fred Whatley, and when we arrived on the platform we took over 30755 *The Red Knight*, relieving the Salisbury men, and pulled up into Salisbury yard to collect the

Urie S15 class 4-6-0 No 502 passing Esher with an up Bournemouth semi-fast in LSWR days. These engines were built for goods service but were used frequently on passenger trains

rest of our train. The guard came up – '55 on and all vacuum fitted'. We got the tip and started off. I had a tender full of briquettes, house brick size, and I can still smell them burning with that tarry tang. [After Porton Tunnel] I picked up the shovel and started firing over the half door. The locomotive was now digging into the bank. She came round to 180lb/sq in – the maximum – and started to blow off. I opened the fire doors and tried to keep her back, but she continued to make steam. She was now round to 190lb/sq in and still making steam. Suddenly I heard a roar: the only thing I can liken it to is that of a jet plane on take-off. She started to prime, and Fred, throwing open the cylinder cocks, shouted, 'Knock her back'. I did not need telling; I closed the dampers and opened the door fully. Still she continued to make steam and was now round to 200lb/sq in. The glass full of water had been thrown out of the chimney, and the half glass of water remaining was bubbling and turning over. I can still see the muck in the glass. [The boiler pressure went up to 220lb/sq in]. I dived into the tender and throwing the briquettes to the back dug down till I came to a load of wet slack. I heaved as much of this as I could on to the fire, and eventually knocked her back as we approached Andover. I can still visualise the rockets being thrown out of her chimney high into the air, with the chalk cliffs on each side

76

of us. At last I managed to hold her around the 160lb/sq in mark. I did not want that experience again! On arrival at Woking the guard came up and asked what the noise was climbing Porton!

Urie followed his N15s with a goods variety, the S15s, which were very similar to the N15s though the cylinders of slightly smaller diameter and the coupled wheels 5ft 7in. A total of 20 engines was built in 1920–21. The choice of a 4-6-0 wheel arrangement for heavy freight locomotives was not common, but it had the advantage that while the heaviest LSWR fast goods trains could be worked easily by six-coupled engines, the leading bogie allowed these small-wheeled engines to be used freely on relief and holiday passenger trains.

Like the N15s, they were modified by Maunsell to improve their steaming, but since their lower pitched boilers did not need such a small chimney they were fitted with the type used on Maunsell's U1 class 2-6-0s. They were very successful engines, and at the time of writing No 506 is undergoing restoration by the Urie S15 Preservation Group for working on the Mid-Hants Railway.

The Urie 4-6-0s were basically very good engines, and it only needed a thorough re-design of the steam circuit to turn them into quite outstanding classes. This is what the new chief mechanical engineer, R. E. L. Maunsell, was to do. It was not a particularly easy task because T. S. Finlayson, the chief draughtsman at Eastleigh, was akin to Joynt of the Great Southern & Western in his dislike of Swindon practices. Holcroft said that he clung to the Urie practices and would never admit that the King Arthurs were any better than Urie's original N15s.

This chapter on Urie engines can be concluded fittingly with another story by Marsh:

I was in the cabin at Nine Elms late in 1947 when a driver came in who had just been handed a 'lost time' ticket by the foreman. The alleged offence had occurred a week or two earlier and the driver could not remember how or why he had lost time. There were a number of almost standard reasons which drivers entered on these tickets . . . He wrote down 'Poor quality coal engine not steaming'. A few minutes later the fireman who had been on this turn came into the cabin and the driver said to him, 'Do you remember that trip I had with you; why did we lose time?' The fireman could not recall much about the incident and agreed with the driver that 'poor quality coal engine not steaming' was the correct reason. Satisfied the driver had a cup of tea. A few minutes later, however, the foreman re-appeared and asked, 'What was the number of the engine?' '30752', replied the driver. Every one in the cabin roared with laughter for 30752 *Linette* was an oil-burner!

7 R. E. L. Maunsell

Richard Maunsell, who was to adopt and revolutionise Urie's 4-6-0 engines, had come from the Great Southern & Western Railway in Ireland to be chief mechanical engineer on the South Eastern & Chatham Railway; when this was amalgamated with the other lines south of the Thames to form the Southern Railway, Maunsell was selected as CME of the new company. The locomotives first produced after Maunsell's appointment to the SECR did not show any of the distinction displayed by his later designs.

Fortunately, Maunsell was well aware of the remarkable capacity displayed by the Great Western engines designed by G. J. Churchward, and he invited to join his staff G. H. Pearson and H. Holcroft from Swindon. The former was to be assistant chief mechanical engineer and works manager at Ashford, while the latter was to plan the extension and reorganisation of the Ashford locomotive, carriage, and wagon shops. In addition to these Great Western men, James Clayton came from the Midland Railway to take over in a few months the position of chief draughtsman.

Soon after his arrival, Pearson suggested to Maunsell that the SECR needed a mixed-traffic 2-6-0 on the lines of the Great Western 43XX class, the design of which Holcroft had worked out on Churchward's instructions. Maunsell agreed and directed Clayton to start on this and on a 2-6-4 tank engine, which Pearson persuaded him would be suitable for passenger traffic, with the advantage that the two classes could have much in common.

The N class 2-6-0, built at Ashford, had a coned boiler barrel 10in diameter, long-travel piston valves with 1½in lap, outside Walschaert valve gear (unlike the GWR), and a considerably higher degree of superheat than used on the GWR. The N class brought the SECR into the front rank of locomotive practice, though Holcroft thought that the adoption of the same boiler for the tender and tank engines was an error; because its size was dictated by the permitted axle loads of the latter, the weight of the full side tanks of which would not allow a heavier boiler. The 2-6-0s as a result were a little 'shy' for steam. This is perhaps a slight digression but it was the success of the Ns which led indirectly to the design of the King Arthurs and the Maunsell S15s.

In March 1924 the need for additional express engines to meet the expansion of the Waterloo services had become urgent. There was an order outstanding for the 10 Drummond 4-6-0s of the G14 (and P14) class to be rebuilt as H15, but the locomotive running department did not want any more mixed-traffic engines. Maunsell decided therefore to rebuild them as express passenger engines similar in general to the Urie N15s, but to

Urie N15 class 4-6-0 No 745 *Tintagel*, fitted with a Maunsell chimney and blastpipe, on a special passenger train of LMS, LNW and Midland stock at Winchfield in 1937

Maunsell King Arthur class 4-6-0 No 454 *Queen Guinevere* working the Atlantic Coast Express on Seaton bank in the 1930s (*Donald R. Barber*)

'Ashfordise' the design by incorporating such N class features as the smokebox arrangement, superheater header, new 20½in by 28in cylinders, long-travel valves, and a boiler pressure of 200lb/sq in. The first to appear was No 453 *King Arthur* in February 1925. It was an immediate success. These Maunsell N15s were among the finest express engines in the country. One can perhaps compare Maunsell's development of the original Urie design with that of Gresley's improvements to Ivatt's large Atlantics on the Great Northern Railway. A handsome cast-metal paper weight model of the engine was sold at Waterloo for a very modest price. I bought and treasured one, but it was stolen alas during the War, and attempts to purchase another were unsuccessful.

The first 10 engines were built at Eastleigh; 30 more were then ordered from the North British Locomotive Company, and these differed from the Eastleigh batch in having Ashford cabs and smokebox doors. Because they were built north of the Border, these latter engines acquired the nickname of 'Scotsmen'. Another 14 followed from Eastleigh in 1925–26.

Holcroft was on the footplate during a remarkable run made by No 451 *Sir Lamorak* from Waterloo to Salisbury with the 11.00am Atlantic Coast Express. This came at the end of a series of tests carried out with King Arthurs by Holcroft in 1925, on Maunsell's instructions. The scheduled time for the journey was 92 minutes, and Holcroft says that before the indicating shelter and gear were taken off, the test engineer wanted another run to get more diagrams at speed, and the driver was asked to work the engine 'a bit heavy'. The result was that Salisbury was reached in 76 minutes – 16 minutes under schedule, at an average start-to-stop speed of 66.1mph. Holcroft adds 'The arrival at Salisbury 16 minutes before time took the station staff unawares, and there were no porters to attend to passengers on arrival. (Those were the days before passengers had to fend for themselves!) Marsh, coming across the log of this trip, found it almost unbelievable:

The nearest I saw this being broken was in about 1950 when the Atlantic Coast Express was re-introduced. Driver Walter Hooper, who was in the top link at Nine Elms and one of the best drivers in the depot, had his own engine, 35012 *United States Lines*, on a trip which was recorded enthusiastically in a magazine. The writer believed that he was going to reach Salisbury in under 70 minutes, but Hooper eased his engine.

Holcroft summarised the King Arthur class as follows:

They were the mainstay of the Southern Railway express passenger services during the Maunsell era. These engines did the job they were designed for in a completely competent manner; they were economical in running, rode well and were easy to maintain. Yet through their very virtues they appeared to me as being prosaic, notwithstanding the romantic names attached to them; one could always anticipate how they would measure up to a job within their capacity.

Though Holcroft did not quite mean this as a compliment, I suppose that no railway company could have asked more of its engines!

Another 15 freight engines were built at Eastleigh in 1927–28. Holcroft calls them an 'Arthurised' version of the Urie S15 class, which differed from the King Arthurs mainly in having coupled wheels of 5ft 7in diameter. They were just as good as the large-wheeled version, and 10 more were built in 1936. I regarded them as the most handsome of the engines that passed my garden (bordering on the Reading–Wokingham line) regularly during the declining years of steam. Jim Marsh, however, had a dismal experience with one of them. He writes:

I remember having a terrible trip on a Maunsell S15 when I was in the No 2 Link with Fred Whatley. We went passenger to Eastleigh to work an up boat train from the Docks to Waterloo. On arrival at Eastleigh we saw the shed foreman who pointed out to us the engine allocated. We got on to the footplate and I made a nice fire, sloping towards the front. When we were ready we pulled up to the signal and waited for our turn to go tender-first to the docks. It was during this movement that we got our first shock, for she had a flat tyre.

We soon discovered that she was loose everywhere, and the boiler front appeared to be detached from the main framing. We got onto the road proper, and I started firing to her over the half door, little and often. She was steaming well and I put on my injector, cutting it fine. Apart from the 'flat' she was not too bad.

Suddenly my injector jumped off. I noticed that the water feed was so loose that it was just swinging about. I switched it over and went across to put on Fred's: that failed to work at all, although it was all right at Eastleigh. I gave mine a couple of clumps with the hammer and it improved slightly. However, a minute or two later it jumped off again. We tied it up with string and then put a piece of wood under it, but to no avail. It kept jumping off and I was losing water, with the result that she started to blow off. I then discovered that the only way that I had any chance of controlling the feed at all was to balance on my left leg and swing my right leg around, holding it in

83

place with my boot. Well, to say the least, it was most difficult firing in such a position, especially with a flat tyre, so for a while Fred changed sides and held the thing in place.

Because of the vibration the engine and tender seemed to be meeting in the middle and my fire started shaking down under the brick arch, so that she soon went off the boil. I closed the back damper and opened the front one wide in an effort to burn fire from the front end and under the brick arch. Owing to the speed and the coal on the footplate I was just shovelling off the floor into the firebox, straight under the door. She was not burning any fire down at the front end, and what I placed under the door was being shifted towards the front and soon it was level with the brick arch. I got the pricker down and tried to pull the fire back, but again to no avail. Consequently she started to drop back and soon I was down to 120–140lb, and so off had to come the injector, and we started sacrificing water for steam. Through Woking, and we were still struggling on with the air filled with coal dust and mountains of coal on the footplate. I had difficulty in standing, let alone working. We had about 120lb of steam and water was down to about an inch in the bottom nut. I was well aware that the slightly opened regulator was keeping it up, and we were still our couple of minutes down.

Eventually we arrived at Waterloo about right time. We had to take the engine home, and I had to shovel about half a ton of coal from the footplate into the tender, and I still had too much fire in the box. On the way, running tender first to Loco, Fred managed to shift most of the fire. Somehow one felt that something had been accomplished. I never worked on an engine again with a flat tyre and I never wanted to!

Something had indeed been accomplished! Through pride in the job a great tradition had been upheld, without expectation of any reward. The efforts of driver and fireman remind one of that other gallant team in the great blizzard of 1881. Marsh had a high opinion of the Maunsell S15s. He continues:

I always found these engines to be simple, efficient, and economical. In the main they steamed well and I enjoyed working on them. A few weeks after the above experience, I was on another boat train with a sister engine, No 30840. Again we went passenger to Eastleigh to pick up our engine, but this time it was as different as chalk from cheese. No 30840 had just come out of the shops and was effectively brand new.

Maunsell Lord Nelson class 4-6-0 No 852 *Sir Walter Raleigh* on a down Bournemouth express at Battledown flyover. This engine was severely damaged by enemy bombs in April 1941

We set back on our train, [at Southampton Docks] only 10 on – a mixture again of bogies and Pullmans – and left with a full head of steam and a pot of water. I started firing to her over the half door, and soon I had to open the door fully as she kept blowing-off. I let the water come down the glass a little in an effort to control her. Through Eastleigh and on towards Winchester, and all the way up the bank her Ross pop safety valves were going zzzzpop, zzzzpop, zzzzpop – I just could not keep her quiet. On approaching the tunnels I made sure that I had let the water come down the glass a little, because I did not want the safety valves going off inside them. Fred came over to my side, remarking on what a good engine she was, and we discussed the type of trains she could have timed. I remember saying, that she would have steamed on a candle!

This account tells us much of the art and craft of the fireman, which required much more skill than the driving of diesel or electric locomotives, let alone the duties of the second man.

Designed for fast or heavy freight trains, the Maunsell S15s were as good as any mixed-traffic 4-6-0s in the country, and as Marsh's description of No 30840 shows, quite as at home on express passenger trains as on the duties for which they were designed. D. L. Bradley writes that on the Portsmouth services they gave such a good account of themselves that many drivers considered them the equal of the 'Schools', 'which was praise indeed.' No 30840 was withdrawn in September 1964.

The project for Maunsell's 4-cylinder Lord Nelson class 4-6-0s actually preceded the construction of the King Arthurs. The expansion of the latter class, when 30 more were ordered from the North British Locomotive Company, was due to the urgent need of express engines for the old LSWR, or Western section of the Southern Railway, which could not await the time required to design and construct the new and powerful engines for the faster and heavier passenger trains visualised.

The type of engine needed was the subject of much discussion between Clayton (by then personal assistant to the cme) and his own assistant, Holcroft. The construction of the Lord Nelsons marked says Holcroft, 'The end of an era during which two groups of locomotives were designed for the Southern Railway, following mainly Ashford and Eastleigh practices respectively.' But the Lord Nelson was definitely 'Southern' in that its design owed comparatively little to either Ashford or Eastleigh and even diverged somewhat from the Churchward practices introduced by Pearson. Holcroft took part in outlining the design as regards the proportions, but he had no part in the details of construction. Given his way the engine would have reflected the detailed design of the Swindon 4-cylinder engines. However, the Nelsons were in Holcroft's opinion perhaps the most reliable, trouble-free, and economical of all Southern locomotives, but he thought they could have been better. Bullied improved them considerably by fitting a modified Lemaître blastpipe, together with a chimney of wide diameter, new cylinders with larger diameter piston valves, and better steam and exhaust passages.

Marsh, voicing the opinion of a good many enginemen, was not particularly impressed with the Nelsons. He wrote:

A lot of people look on Nelsons most affectionately: a good looking engine, a big engine, but with their four cylinders they never measured up to my expectations. I have heard of many stories of what they did before the War, but I never saw them do anything spectacular. A lot has been written about the Bullieds throwing sparks out of their chimneys, but a Nelson at night looked like a firework display, with rockets like stair rods! I must admit that they timed the trains when they had the steam and would make up lost time, but they did not do so easily as a Bullied Pacific. Besides, they were much more difficult to fire, and if they went off the boil for some reason or other they could, particularly with an inexperienced fireman, be most difficult to handle. I remember many drivers saying how when leaving Waterloo they would put on the injector and leave it. I used to like to see the water down an inch from the top nut, and then with a good fire you would have proper superheat.

As regards firing them, I suppose it would be fair to say that the Eastleigh firemen had the edge on the Nine Elms fireman, because they used Nelsons more than we did. The problem with a Nelson was the shape of its firebox. It was 10ft 6in long and about 3ft wide. The firebox dipped under the door, rose towards the centre, and dipped quite sharply towards the tubeplate. Holding one's hand back uppermost and slightly curved produces roughly the shape. Firing a Nelson one closed the firebox doors half way, put up a small half flap attached by a short chain, and fired through a throat plate. The aperture was quite small and we used to have the fire level with the half flap. A Nelson did not like too much against the tube plate and firing 10ft 6in was quite a job. The brick arch was quite low and, if not careful it was easy to get a knob or two stuck at the entrance just under the brick arch, and nothing more could be passed over it. Sometimes I would put a nice couple of pieces of coal in the shovel with the intention of knocking a piece of fire out of the way, rather like playing bowls. But this never worked out; it always caused a further obstruction, so that unless the fire were levelled one could not get at the front of the box. So down had to come the fire-irons – the short or long pricker, depending on the position. However, getting a 12ft pricker down from the tender on a moving engine was quite an art, and putting it back was equally difficult. I remember on one occasion just after passing Woking I threw a pricker up on the tender and it went over the side causing potentially dangerous sparks from the third rail. Most drivers frowned on the use of fire-irons unless absolutely necessary. This was of course a correct attitude, because the art of firing is to use the shovel correctly – fire-irons too often cause clinker.

Excessive use of the blower was always frowned on. It was all right when used while standing still to keep the smoke back or to make steam, and when entering a tunnel, but not to obtain steam on the road. Most of the old drivers said that there was no way other than the beat of the engine of obtaining more blast on a fire, and that using the blower only wasted steam into the atmosphere. They were probably right.

If one was spare, one might have the particularly nasty job of cleaning the tubes and superheater tubes, for which we were allowed two hours. It was much easier if the engine had no fire; if she was in steam, one first had to ensure that the firebox doors were closed. The superheater tubes were not too bad as the soot and ash could be blasted out with an air gun, but the ordinary tubes were a much worse proposition, particularly on a big locomotive. For this task there was a rod about 20ft long and a little thinner than a pencil. At one end was a small wooden bobble like a door handle, and at the end was a small hole in which one tied the piece of wire that actually cleaned the tubes. Imagine trying to clean a couple of hundred tubes, guiding this thin rod into each. After a while, if the engine was in steam, the rod started to get hot, and sometimes the tubes were so bad that the wire got stuck in them. I think this was the worst job on the railway, though an essential one. After a few years Polish staff were employed to clean the superheaters, but firemen occasionally got the job of cleaning the ordinary ones.

I think I was a bit of a railway snob, for though I did not mind what engine I worked on. We used to get a lot of duties called 'P and D' (preparing and disposing of engines). One could be engaged on such duties for a week, or three days in a week.

On turn in particular was without doubt the worst P & D duty in the depot – the disposing of the last Weymouth. The engine for the last Weymouth was always a Nelson. [Arrival back at Waterloo was 10.59pm]. Because the engine had been on the road for something like 15 hours, there was always what looked like a box of fire. When relieving at Waterloo I used to get the fire-irons down while in the station and throw the fire up on one side. Very often the fire was less than two inches thick, but the red-hot clinker would be over a foot thick, almost level with the firehole doors – try putting a dart into a box of clinker!

We were allowed 75 minutes to dispose of a Nelson, but when in this condition it was impossible, and I would have to go round to the foreman and explain to him that the work on her would take longer than the allotted time. The smokebox was always cleaned first to keep the stays and tubes from leaking. On many occasions after getting the Nelson off the last Weymouth up to the shed, I would (having closed the firebox doors) open the smokebox door and see a wall of red-hot ash. One had to jump back quickly before it fell on you. After completing the smokebox, there came the nightmare of the fire. I had already thrown the fire up on one side and by this time the left-hand side of the fire was out. But I now had to dig down 12 to 18 inches of clinker. My Great Western 8ft shovel was all right for the first six to seven ft but after that I would have to use the long fire-irons and long clinker shovels. These shovels were about 11ft 6in long (for a Nelson firebox was about 18ft 6in in length). Some of them had solid handles which made them very heavy, while others had hollow handles which, though much lighter, soon became very hot and would often go out of shape. More often than not one would have three or four long shovels on the go. Some Nelsons had drop grates, though personally I never used them. The drop grate was about eight ft from the door, and quite often when it was used a piece of clinker would get stuck in the works, so that one could not close the grate and the fire had to come out.

After finishing the fire one had to go underneath to do the ashpans – crawling about in the dark with a paraffin torch lamp and a rake, oil dripping on you, clambering over other heaps of red-hot ash, fire, and clinker, sometimes in two to three inches of water, boots sizzling or soaking. Then back one would go on to the footplate to ensure that there was sufficient water in the boiler. The task ended with sweeping the floor and putting the 'pep' over the floor and the boiler front of the cab, for I always liked to get onto a clean footplate.

On this turn a Nelson did about 330 miles. I once spoke to a Bournemouth fireman about the state of the fire and smokebox. He told me that because of the extra duty on arrival at Weymouth the fireman there did not have time to clean the fire, and certainly not the smokebox. If she was not steaming well the fireman would sometimes run the dart through the fire and pull out a couple of large lumps of clinker. With the fire in such a state one can well understand why some of the crews had bad journeys, especially coming up the bank from Southampton, but as I have said I was lucky and had good trips on this turn, and can remember many occasions on which we arrived at Waterloo, even after the altered timing had knocked three minutes off the schedule.

I suspect that what Marsh calls luck was really the result of his own very competent firing. The above passage gives a very vivid description of how unpleasant a task it could be in disposing of an engine which arrived in poor condition after a long run. Marsh had an unpleasant experience of a Nelson in bad condition.

In 1954 I had a spare day and was booked to work with Bert 'Slicer' Knowles. We signed on in the depot about 4.00pm and collected 30865 *Sir John Hawkins*, which we got ready and went up to Waterloo tender-first to work the 5.30pm to Bournemouth. I had never worked with Bert before and thought I had better be on my best behaviour, so I arrived early and started to make up the fire slowly and properly as per the training manual. Going to Waterloo, I noticed that she was slowly falling back, but I thought she would be all right when we started. The guard came up to report '11 on' and stopping at Basingstoke, Winchester, and Eastleigh, where we would be relieved. We started off, and as we cleared Westminster Bridge she had a full head. I put on the injector, just seeing the water in the top nut, when suddenly the windows were obliterated with wet soot and the brakes started clicking ominously. Bert shouted 'Knock her back!' I did not need to for she was already going off the boil. I was down to about 190lb, and going through Vauxhall she chucked out nearly a boiler full of water. Bert opened the cocks. 'Knock her back, Marsho', he shouted. I closed the dampers, opened the firebox doors, and switched off the injector. He called out, 'I think I will stop at Loco Junction and ask for another engine.' I replied, 'How can you? You have only just started, and if you stop there at this time of day you will stop the railway.' 'OK', he said, 'we will carry on and see how we do.' He eased her off through Clapham Junction, and I was down to about 160lb and an inch of water. On opening up for the rise to Earlsfield she again started to prime. We wanted steam and water, and if we got more than an inch in the glass she threw it out. I knocked her back further and we started to get round the 140lb mark. Coming up to Surbiton we were losing time badly; the water was getting very low and I only had about 120lb of steam. Bert wrote out a note asking for another engine at Basingstoke. We went through Woking 20 minutes late, having taken 48 minutes instead of 28. Bert shut the regulator. I had the injector on and was standing on tiptoe, but could not see the water in the boiler. I wanted to try the drain cock, but was frightened in case it was too low, and I did not want to waste any for I was down to 100lb.

Bert came over to my side and threw his note to the platform staff. He then opened out the regulator and the water came into view. I switched off the injector for the hump round to Brookwood and got her back to 110lb of steam, but the water was still low, and the only thing that made the water cover the lead plugs was the regulator lifting the water. Just past Brookwood there was a 15mph speed restriction, where Bert closed the regulator and let her run. I slapped on the injector, but even with the regulator closed I still could not see any water and was now down to 90lb. After clearing the speed restriction I put the injector on, and we continued on our merry way. We eventually stopped in Basingstoke 35 minutes late, with water out of sight and 90lb of steam. While our relief uncoupled I put on the other injector, but it was at least two minutes before the water came into sight, and we were down to 65lb of steam when she moved off. We then took over a Remembrance and plodded on to Eastleigh. What a different trip up! We had a brand new Schools just out of the Shops, and the parcels train that we returned with came up the bank like an express.

The next day I was at Basingstoke waiting to work a train to London when I saw this thing approaching very slowly. I could not make out what it was; it was a blackish, muddish, green mottled coloured engine with its windows covered in soot. As she stopped I saw it was No 30865. The fireman, an Eastleigh man, recognised me and called me over. I went to see if I could give him a hand. He said 'You had this one yesterday and came off here. Why?' I replied, 'The same as you; priming.' 'The so-and-so foreman told me,' he said, 'that there was nothing wrong with her and that the London fireman did not know how to fire her. Wait till I get back home!' He left Basingstoke with water out of sight and 90lb of steam. How he got up the bank I will never know. It appears that after we came off at Basingstoke, instead of the Basingstoke staff washing her out, they just sent her on to Eastleigh light engine, and Eastleigh did not wash her out either.

The Remembrance class, which Marsh mentions, were Maunsell's rebuild of the London Brighton & South Coast Railway 4-6-4 tank engines into 4-6-0 tender engines. Holcroft regarded them as very useful locomotives on the Western Section, but about equivalent to the Urie N15s.

Although he did not care for them, Marsh had other and pleasant experiences of Nelsons. In the summer of 1954 he was with driver Fred Whatley in the No 2 Link. Each week on Monday, Wednesday, and Friday they worked the down Normandy Coast Express, 9.00pm from Waterloo to Southampton Old Docks. They were always given a Nelson, and turning the engine at Southampton worked back with it on the Mail train leaving Southampton Town at 12.40am. Marsh continues:

On one Monday trip No 30859 *Lord Hood* behaved beautifully. We had a mixture of 12 ordinary bogies and Pullmans, and a couple of vans, about 460 tons. We arrived in the Docks on time, uncoupled our train, and put into the tiny locomotive yard at the Town. Fred oiled her up, I ran the dart through the fire and prepared her for the return trip. I left the doors open, filled up the boiler, and knocked the steam back. As we had some time to pass after getting the coal down and taking water we 'screwed her down' and went to the cabin for our break. We had been in the cabin for about an hour when she let out a mighty roar, blowing-off at the safety valves. It was then about midnight, dark and quiet in the surrounding area. I went immediately to put the injector on in an attempt to knock her back, but she still had a boiler full and there is only so much that you can get into a boiler. There was a high wall surrounding the tiny yard, and just behind it a row of terraced cottages. Suddenly, only a few feet away, an irate male resident threw up a bedroom window and gave me a right mouthful. I tried to apologise, but my apologies were doing no good, and he was going to report me to my Guv'nor. At this moment one of the ocean liners, leaving on a late tide, let out a full-blooded blast on her siren. 'What about that?' I said, 'He is making more noise than me.' 'Oh,' he replied, 'that's different; I can sleep through that.' Not to be outdone, I retorted, 'They can hear that in Winchester.' Fred could hear the argument, and coming out made the peace, and the complainant went back to bed. We then went back to our train and had a good trip working home, with her behaving beautifully up the bank. This train, strangely, was the only steam-hauled turn that stopped at Vauxhall. We were relieved there, and I remember that the relieving crew used to sign on at 3.49am. I have done this turn as well.

On the Wednesday night we had No 30859 again and she was still in good nick. Again a good trip down, but still a job to keep her quiet. When we arrived in Southampton, Fred did the oiling and said, 'You will have to keep her quiet tonight Jimmer; we don't want

92

any more complaints.' As on the previous trip, I ran the dart through the fire and put some nice knobs under the brick arch. Then I became cocky, for which I was to pay for later. I dug down into the tender, and from the brick arch to the firebox doors I filled her up with wet slack. I left only one notch of the dampers open and filled the boiler up to the whistle. Then, leaving the firebox doors open, we went and had our supper. All was nice and quiet while we were eating our supper, and we were congratulating ourselves that she was behaving herself. About an hour later we got on to the footplate, and then discovered why she had been so quiet. Between the brick arch and the firebox doors the fire was actually out. I opened the dampers fully and then jumped down into the pit to have a look at the ashpans. I tried to throw out some of the slack but time was running short. I picked up the pricker and tried to push some of the wet slack down the front of the firebox, at the same time pulling back some of the fire under the brick arch. I had the blower full on, and while standing still she was making steam, but I knew that once we started with only half a fire we were going to be in trouble. We got back on our train, and during the whole time we were in the platform I was using dart and pricker with the blower full on. We left Southampton blowing-off and water up to the whistle. I knew that we could manage Eastleigh, but we also knew that she was not going to make any steam on the road. On the way past Swaythling and St Denys it was all pricker and dart, but as I thought that a good boiler of water would take us to Eastleigh, I did not have to put on the injector. Nevertheless, she would not make steam, and en route continually dropped back and went off the boil. We eventually ran into Eastleigh with about 120–140lb/sq in. All the time in the station I had the blower full on, and again it was pricker and dart. I soon had a full head of steam and a boiler of water, and while the platform staff loaded us with the mails, I knew that we had some 10 to 15 minutes' respite. After leaving Eastleigh we were into the bank proper. Fortunately we did not need the injector between Eastleigh and Winchester, but on the way up the bank she again dropped back and I was again on the pricker. Running into Winchester, we were starting to make a little headway. We had another ten minutes or so at Winchester, and again it was blower full on and me still on the pricker. We left there with a full head and a pot of water. For the first time the whole of the firebox had a proper fire; but, with the constant use of pricker and dart, I had made quite a bit of dirt. On approaching Micheldever she started to make steam on the road; so I got her well over and put the injector on while running. From then on she was all right. Fred fortunately had a sense of humour and took all this in good part. 'You will never do that again, Jim old bean,' he laughed.

I can recall the 'Great Smog' of 1952. During part of that week I was on the 3.30pm Waterloo to Bournemouth, and up with the last Weymouth, arriving back at Waterloo at 10.59pm. We were always allocated a Nelson down and up on that turn, except that once because of the traffic chaos we once had a West Country. Two days out of the three we never arrived at Bournemouth but were relieved as we ran into Pokesdown, where we walked across to the up platform to take over our charge. The reason for this was that the motive power authorities at Bournemouth knew that if we arrived there Fred would have demanded his meal break, and that would have caused further delays. So it was off one footplate and on to another, eating our sandwiches as we went. The amazing thing about those ten days was that although one could not see more than 20 to 30yd ahead, once outside the London area (Woking in effect) trains were being timed and time was even being made up. I remember one driver coming in and saying that the first time he saw the stars was at Micheldever. During those ten days a Bournemouth fireman gave me a very useful tip. He said: 'When you are looking for signals, put your head just outside the window and look over the top of the chimney, and you will see them all.' He was right, though at times I do not think I could see the chimney! He also told me that between Worting and Woking, as the signals were fairly evenly spaced out, you should fire to the engine as fast as you could up to the count of 30, then close the doors and poke your head out of the window, which would give sufficient time to get used to the changing light and weather conditions. I found this invaluable information, and I never missed a signal. The first time I tried it I was surprised at the amount of work one could do in a few seconds, for after firing there was always time for a quick sweep of the floor and a check of the injectors, without delaying the look out at the side to see the signals. On the evening that we had the West Country, the exhaust steam as usual hung down on Fred's side so that he was in a complete smog. After leaving Winchester Fred switched out the lights on the footplate, for it was surprising how much glare the small electric bulbs gave. I lit the paraffin gauge lamp and used that. 'Don't worry about the steam, Jim,' said Fred, 'just see those signals.' We were really going quickly, but we saw all the signals up to Woking. Just past Woking he missed one, though I saw it and said, 'OK'. However, as he had missed it he wanted further corroboration, and put on the brake. We pulled into West Byfleet very very slowly, for the only way we knew it was a station was that it was a little lighter. A porter on the down platform called out to us and gave us a green light. I could only just make out a dim shadow and a very dim light. 'OK to Surbiton, mate,' he called out. We arrived in Waterloo about 20 minutes late, and that was only due to congestion in the London area.

Maunsell's masterpiece was the last of his designs, the brilliant 3-cylinder Schools class 4-4-0s. They were the most powerful engines of this wheel arrangement ever constructed in Europe, perhaps in the world. Holcroft regarded them as 'the best value for money ever put on rails.' The cylinders, motion, and bogie embodied many parts common with the Nelsons, while the boiler was a shortened version of the King Arthur type, but with a higher boiler pressure. Holcroft said that at a pinch they could tackle jobs usually allotted to Nelsons, and that they could exceed the haulage power of the King Arthurs. Forty were built between 1930 and 1935. They were most handsome, though Bullied did nothing to improve their appearance by fitting half of them with his modified Lemaître blastpipe and wide diameter chimney.

All were named after public schools and the Southern Railway did its best to establish a relationship between each school and its engine. At the time of the centenary celebrations of Wellington College in 1959 No 30902 *Wellington* was assigned by Southern Region (following the tradition of its predecessor) to haul trains on the Redhill–Reading line, stopping at Crowthorne, which had been named Wellington College in South Eastern and SECR days. It gave me considerable pleasure to see this beautifully turned-out engine, named after my old school, running through the cutting at the end of my garden. No 902 has the distinction of figuring in one of the stained-glass windows of the Wellington College chapel.

No disparagement of Maunsell's magnificent work is intended if I finish this chapter on a minor note though Hecate, Greek goddess of the underworld, might be offended at such a

95

disparaging description! She was a goddess who apparently fascinated Lieutenant Colonel H. F. Stephens, who was responsible for so many light railways, and who obtained *Hecate*, in the shape of a 0-8-0 tank engine from Hawthorn Leslie & Co for the goods services which were planned over the projected extension of his Kent & East Sussex Railway to Maidstone. Unfortunately the extension never materialised and *Hecate*, precluded by weight from operating elsewhere on his systems, was kept resplendent in Great Eastern blue and copper and brass an object of worship which was steamed once a month, presumably as the mechanical equivalent of a burnt offering. Colonel Stephens resolutely refused to sell *Hecate*, but after his death in 1931 the locomotive was acquired by the Southern Railway, reconditioned and numbered 949 (later BR No 30949). It was noted that its reversing lever needed modification because it was pulled back to travel forward, and pushed forward to move backwards. It does not appear that this was ever carried out, for Jim Marsh noted that 'When in full fore gear she went backwards and when in reverse gear she went forwards. She certainly lived up to her name, but if one was unaware of her peculiarity it could be quite dangerous. She was often known as 'The Bug', or 'Mullings' Shunter', after the shed foreman at Nine Elms.'

8 O. V. S. Bulleid

I have dealt in detail elsewhere with the development, troubles, and rebuilding of Bulleid's pacific locomotives. Despite the severe criticisms levelled at their design, there is no doubt about the fascination, and indeed affection, which these controversial engines inspired among footplatemen and amateur enthusiasts alike. Fitters regarded them in their unrebuilt form with the utmost disfavour. A few months before he died R. L. Curl, a senior locomotive draughtsman under Bulleid and President of the Bulleid Society, wrote to me giving some of his recollections of Bulleid. They include the following:

> I feel I was fortunate in working for the great O.V.B. and enjoying his company after retirement, and the following twelve years of correspondence . . . When he came to Eastleigh, he was received with respect, even awe, amounting to fear almost! J. Munns, workshops superintendent said, 'Give him what he wants. If he wants the chimney on the bloody tender we'll put it there.'
>
> The design staff – nothing new since the Schools – were not of the calibre he should have had. For instance, when the chief draughtsman gave me the job of coupling and connecting rods, wheels and axles, he said: 'I should get out the Nelsons and Schools and see what we did there.' Bulleid was amused when I told him this years later. It was rumoured that at a meeting discussing the engine building programme they drummed on the table and chanted: 'We want Lord Nelsons'. Bulleid insisted that he was not building engines 15 years old.
>
> I must have been the only draughtsman to say to him, 'No, Sir, you can't do that.' He was looking at my outside connecting rod on the board and suggested a dust cover on the big end to stop the

97

ingress of grit and sand. I prepared two schemes, as I always tried to do; one was a cast-aliminium cover which would screw onto a face, suitably secured, the other in charcoal iron, secured by a jubilee clip. 'No! No! No!' he said. 'I want one that will press on.' 'But, Sir, you can't do that; if it came off at speed it would wipe people off their feet, or cut off their heads, going through a station. If you press it on, it could fly off.' 'But I have them on my car hubs.' 'Yes, Sir, but your car hub is rotating axially, except for a slight deflection of the tyre, but this is at 12in radius at 400rpm.' He actually brought in one of his car hubs – I still have it as a reminder. He was reluctant to abandon the idea, but he did. I feel he had confidence in me; perhaps more than in himself! But you see any other draughtsman would have given him what he wanted – with what possible consequences! But it is inexplicable to me that he should have slipped up like that, with his master mind; or was I wrong?

I feel his Leader would have been a totally different story had his staff been worth their salt and guided him.

Above all Oliver Bulleid was retiring, mild, never upset (or at least never showed it), and had a strong Christian faith. He was nurtured in the Anglican faith, but work and residence on the Continent, especially in Turin where he engineered the Exhibition, drew him to the Roman Catholic faith, in which he was devout. 'After all,' he said, 'we owe our very civilisation to Rome.' I confess he has influenced my life considerably. I still miss him after 10 years . . . I have written the foregoing hoping it will give you even a closer knowledge than you have of him.

This is a remarkable picture of a brilliant engineer, who could inspire great affection in those who got to know him. A genius in any field tends perhaps to be slightly impracticable, and Curl's letter brings out the responsibilities of draughtsmen to examine brilliant ideas and to point to difficulties that may arise in their implementation. Had this been done it was conceivable that many of the troubles that afflicted Bulleid's engines would never have arisen.

Marsh's admiration for Bulleid's Pacifics probably represents the opinion of many if not most of the footplatemen who handled them. He writes: 'A lot has been written about the expensive maintenance, and the coal, water, and oil consumption. There is no doubt that they were heavier on oil and maintenance and that sometimes they used more coal than conventional engines, but look at their performance. I think that most people agree that a Rolls Royce uses more fuel than other cars. In my opinion, these were the Rolls Royce of locos.'

There were two different versions of Bulleid pacifics, 30 engines of the Merchant Navy class and 110 of the lighter variety, described more or less in accordance with the names of the locomotives as the West Country or Battle of Britain classes. They all looked so much the same that it was not always obvious which was which at a casual glance. Nevertheless, there was considerable difference between the two, as the following dimensions show:

	Merchant Navy	*Light Pacific*
Cylinders (3)	18in × 24in	16⅜in × 24in
Piston Valves	11in	10in
Grate Area	48.5sq ft	38.5sq ft
Weight	92½ tons	86 tons

The boiler diameter and length, working pressure, and coupled wheel diameter were the same for both classes.

The 30 locomotives of the Merchant Navy class (or 'Packets', as they were nicknamed) were delivered in three batches of 10. The first batch entered traffic in 1941–42, the second in 1944–45, and the third after Nationalisation, in 1948–49. In the light of experience with the first 10 engines, certain modifications were incorporated in the later ones. The 110 West Country/Battle of Britain class (the 'Lightweights') were built from 1945 to 1951, the last 40 appearing after Nationalisation. All the Merchant Navy class were rebuilt between 1956 and 1959. Of the light pacifics, 60 were rebuilt from 1957 to 1961.

After rebuilding, the engines had an appearance which conformed to the lines adopted for the British Railways family of locomotives. They were extremely handsome, and very similar to Riddles' Britannia class, except for the wide chimney and Bulleid wheels. Yet the rebuilt engines were still primarily Bulleid's design, with his magnificent boiler and most of the other

Driver Fred Whatley in the cab of Merchant Navy class Pacific No 35011 *General Steam Navigation* in 1954 (*J. Marsh*)

important features. The troublesome valve gear, oil sump, air-smoothed casing, and steam reverser were the principal cause of casualties before rebuilding.

The locomotives in their original form were at their best magnificent performers, and during the Interchange Trials of 1948 though the Bulleid engines were more extravagant than their rivals in coal and water consumption, the late Cecil J. Allen was able to write of them: 'The most uniform standard of performance throughout the tests was put up by the Southern engines, behind which it was a joy to travel.'

Marsh has many stories relating to his favourite engines. He relates, for instance, an amusing incident connected with a Bournemouth working starting about 1950 and of his own experience with the same service some four years later. He says that at that time there was a very senior Admiralty civil servant who lived at Winchester and who travelled daily to Waterloo on the train which left Bournemouth West at 7.20am. If the train was more than two minutes late at Waterloo he registered a complaint. The management therefore put a good engine on to this train, which stayed on it for months.

The complete turn for this working started with the 2.40am paper train from Waterloo to Bournemouth. The engine turned at Branksome to work the 7.20am from Bournemouth West, stopping at Bournemouth Central, Boscombe, Pokesdown, Christchurch, New Milton, Brockenhurst, Southampton Central, and Winchester. There was a certain driver at Nine Elms who had been taken off this turn, in his own words, 'for speeding'. Marsh writes:

On this particular day he had 34061 *73 Squadron*, and for some unknown reason he was about 30 minutes late at Worting Junction. He later showed me his 'charge sheet'. He travelled from Worting Junction to Queen's Road (where he was stopped by the guard), a distance of 48 miles in 32 minutes, or 90mph. The guard thought the train was a 'runaway' and going round Clapham Junction applied the brakes hard. The driver was trying unsuccessfully 'to blow it off', so he stopped at Queen's Road. I remember him saying, 'Ah, the guard got scared.' The charge sheet alleged (how I do not know) that his estimated speed through Woking was 108mph. The driver retorted: 'Ah, but they should have seen me at Fleet!' He finished his days on the Nine Elms goods yard on the shunting diesels.

Marsh's own experience on this working was in 1954 with driver Fred Whatley. The same eminent civil servant still lived at Winchester and still travelled on the same train. On this occasion the engine provided for the turn was an unfortunate selection. He writes:

The engine was West Country No 34011 *Tavistock*. Unfortunately a spark arrester had been fitted in the smokebox; though in fact it was just a sheet of metal bolted between the tubeplate and the blastpipe. The result was that she just would not steam. Fred and I had this turn with 34011 for a whole week, which was a bit unusual. For the return journey the train always comprised 12 bogies, loaded to capacity with commuters, so we had over 400 tons behind us. On this trip from Bournemouth West to Southampton it was not too bad, though the engine steadily dropped back until we were usually down to 150–160lb of steam and 1½ inches of water in the gauge glass. We would leave Southampton with about 200lb of steam (although she was at that time pressed to 250lb/sq in) and three-quarters of a glass of water. On a typical occasion, when we started climbing the long haul to Winchester, I was firing as per rule book and had about eight inches of fire all over the box so that I could get as much blast on it as possible. She used hardly any coal, which was no wonder with that arrester in the smokebox! We arrived at Winchester with the blower full on and working like mad to get a few pounds more steam; but even so we left there with only half a glass of water and 150–160lb of steam. The engine got stuck in and we were doing our best, but gradually I was sacrificing water for steam, and on getting over the top of the bank at Litchfield I was down to 110lb of steam and was standing on tiptoes to see the water on the glass. The only thing that was keeping the water over the lead plugs was the slightly open regulator, but it was surprising that the engine was still pulling. There was a clicking in the brake, which sounded ominous, but Fred said, 'Provided the brake holds we will be OK.' We went over the flyover at Worting with the slightly open regulator still keeping the water just above the plugs. Now, with the easier running, the engine flew. I never had more than 130–150lb and 1½ inches of water in the glass, but we were in London on time! Many of the crews were complaining aobut the steaming of this locomotive and Fred went and saw the 'Guvnor'. The latter said that he had many complaints, but he did not know what there was to complain about as everyone was timing the train. This same engine continued on the train, therefore, until a better one came out of the shops.

There are three things that strike one from this account. The first is the remarkable competence of the Southern enginemen in keeping time with such a poor-steaming engine; the second is the astounding ability of the engine to perform so well with such a ghastly handicap inflicted on its steaming; the third is the inexplicable decision by someone to continue with this spark arrester in spite of consistent reports about the effect on the steaming. Its use is the all the more extraordinary in that a spark arrester designed at Brighton had been fitted in 1948 to No 34034 *Honiton*, and an LMS pattern had been tried on No 34033 *Chard*. Both had resulted in such poor steaming that they had been removed.

Marsh's most memorable trip on a Bulleid Pacific was in 1953.

In the summer of 1953 I overheard a heated discussion in the cabin at Nine Elms between drivers Charlie Partridge and Alf Hurley, the latter being the driver of the Churchill funeral train. Hurley was telling other crews that he had timed a passenger train from Salisbury to London in full fore gear, the engine being a Bulleid. Partridge was convinced that this was impossible because the fireman would not be able to keep pace with the fire, the boiler would not be able to maintain the water, and the engine would not be able to obtain sufficient speed in full gear. The controversy went on for several months, many people holding different views. To be honest, I was a 'don't know'.

On 8 October 1953, I started work at Nine Elms at 3.30am. We had West Country No. 34005 *Barnstaple*, and worked the Waterloo train stopping at all stations to Salisbury, arriving there at about 8.40am.

The return journey was a West of England express, leaving Salisbury at 9.33am. Waiting on the platform, I saw No. 35004 *Cunard White Star Line* arrive. Only a few moments after leaving Salisbury at 9.33am I noticed that Fred Whatley was having a bit of difficulty with the reverser. I had a good fire and plenty of water and was not bothered. Just prior to the tunnel, Fred came over to my side and said, 'I'm having a little trouble with the reverser; I'll pull her up when we are through to the other side.' It was dark on the footplate in the tunnel and we did not have the lighting on. After getting to the other side, Fred was still having difficulty, and he told me that he thought the steam reverser pipe had broken because he could not pull up the lever. I went over to his side and just below the name plate I could see a whisp of steam, presumably from a fractured pipe. He then asked me for a piece of paper. I then reminded him of the discussion between Charlie Partridge and Alf Hurley some months before. I added, 'You got involved and said it couldn't be done; now is the time to see. Let's have a go.' He replied, 'OK, you are the fireman and have got to do the work. If you don't mind, I don't, and we will try.'

For the first time I then opened the firebox doors. The crack, crack, crack, from the exhaust was deafening – like a heavy calibre machine gun. The fire was bouncing and the noise almost unbelievable. I started to use the automatic fire doors in an effort to cut down the noise, though usually I did not use them at all. I allowed the water to come down the glass about an inch from the top nut. The needle was bang on 280lb of steam, just below blowing-off, with a white feather from the safety-valves. Fred was doing all he could to spare me too much work. I continued firing up the bank, and to my surprise she was doing better than I expected. I closed the dampers to one notch to protect my fire, and she tore up Porton. Down into Andover, and we stopped a minute late. We decided to take on more water, as we did not know what to expect later. Fred went to have a look at the front end, but he could not do anything. I jumped down and loosened off the coupling a turn, because if he had not stopped right we were in trouble, because there was no way we could reverse. Fortunately we got away first time. We left Andover two minutes late. I was still firing quietly and was not overworked. The water was still an inch from the top nut and she was still bang on 280lb of steam. Round Worting Junction we had dropped another minute, so we were now three minutes down. Fred eased the regulator and she thundered through Basingstoke with the fire like a huge jelly. I still kept a rather big fire in her as we usually got a severe signal check approaching Woking, sometimes stopping, to allow a Portsmouth electric to cross, and I did not want to get caught with too little fire. Through Brookwood and round the corner, and to our surprise all the signals were green. Fred opened her up a bit and she roared through Woking, turning a few heads to say the least. Also, to our surprise, we had picked up our three minutes and were now right on time. We arrived at Waterloo at exactly 11.08am. I had a little too much fire in the box, which did not make me popular with the relief fireman, who had to clean the fire.

Having regard to the coal-eating reputation of the unrebuilt Bulleid pacifics, this was a most remarkable run. It disproved driver Partridge's arguments, because Marsh easily kept pace with the fire and was not exhausted. The boiler did its job magnificently and there was no difficulty over the speed.

It is interesting to compare this run with one I wrote of elsewhere when Bulleid made a footplate trip on a Nelson from Victoria to Dover. On his instructions the engine was driven in full gear up Grosvenor Road bank out of Victoria, and then at 40–50% cut-off for the rest of the way to Dover. Along the straight between Tonbridge and Ashford the regulator was kept wide open and both injectors working to keep the water level in sight. Speeds were between 90mph and 95mph, and when the engine reached Dover the fireman was exhausted but Bulleid was delighted.

But Marsh's feat raises more important questions. The unmodified Bulleid Pacifics were noted for being great consumers of coal, and in another book I have written: 'The rebuilds consumed noticeably less coal and water. The high consumption of the originals caused coaling difficulties at the motive power depots. Although the tenders held five tons, it was almost standard practice for engines to take more coal immediately before leaving a depot. Nearly a ton would be burned in building up the fire before departure, and unless the engine had the coal stacked to the brim there might not be sufficient to cover both outward and return journeys. Engines working the Bournemouth Belle for instance from Waterloo to Bournemouth West and then going on to Branksome to turn, would frequently have to make a light trip to Bournemouth Central for more coal to get the Belle safely back to Waterloo. Commenting on this, Marsh writes: 'We regularly had return trips to Bournemouth and back with these engines and had plenty of coal for the 225-mile round trip to Bournemouth West.' Regarding the astounding run described above Marsh says of his coal, 'We had plenty left, and this engine had come up from Exeter – 170 miles.' He adds, 'Although I have never done it, I have spoken to Salisbury men who have filled the firebox with coal on leaving Nine Elms and who have not, so they told me, picked up the shovel again before Salisbury. I have on many occasions when feeling lazy, filled up the firebox on a Merchant Navy and sat down from Winchester to London without touching the shovel again. I was with Tom Smaldon with one on the up Atlantic Coast Express from Salisbury, when the fireman ran in with such a box of coal and fire that we decided to see how far she would go without touching the shovel. I actually sat down from Salisbury to Woking Station. If I had put in another four to five cwt of coal, and we had not been checked, we could have gone all the way to Waterloo.'

The explanation may well be that much more skill was required in firing the unmodified Bulleid pacifics than is generally supposed. They were so easy to fire that even with a young and inexperienced fireman the driver did not need to look anxiously at the pressure gauge, and it is likely that many firemen realised and learned the skills that were necessary to economise in coal or to meet an emergency. There must have been some such explanation because Marsh's evidence is so strong.

In his criticism of the Bulleid engines, Marsh writes. 'In my opinion the worst aspects about Bulleid engines were firstly the way the exhaust steam and smoke failed to clear away and hung down on one side of the cab or the other, and secondly the steam reverser. If only a conventional reverser had been fitted I feel there would have been a lot less trouble with the gear chains. I have been with drivers who have pulled these engines right up in the middle and have felt the tender sitting back into the train. If they had only put the lever over a little, the engine would have run better and more smoothly, and the valve gear would have probably lasted longer.'

Interference with visibility caused by steam and smoke was never cured until the locomotives were rebuilt without the air-smoothed casing and with normal smoke deflectors fitted. The rebuilt engines did have screw reversing gear, but even with this it is doubtful whether the chain gear would have been satisfactory, because the wear of pins and holes, and also of the intermediate sprocket wheel teeth, effectively lengthened the chains. By the time for general overhaul, the longer chain could have stretched as much as six inches.

The well-known liability of the Bulleid pacifics to slip led to Marsh relating the following rather extraordinary incident.

In 1953 we used to run many specials to Southampton Docks, for this was still the heyday of the liners. We also used to run a number of troop trains to and from the docks, because movements to and from destinations overseas were still undertaken mainly by troopships. Quite often we would go round to West London (GWR) and collect 12 to 14 bogies, or take the empty stock back there from the Docks. I remember Gerry Sartin, a driver in the No 2 Link, telling me how in 1953 he went passenger to Eastleigh and took West Country No. 34006 *Bude*, to the Docks, where he was to collect 14 ex-Midland stock bogies and take them to West London and on to Brent. *Bude* had only been out of the shops a couple of months and was in first class condition. Gerry had an uneventful trip with his 14 bogies until he arrived in the Brent region. There was a steep bank where any train with over 30 goods wagons had to have a banking locomotive at the rear. When he arrived at this bank he was stopped by a signal. After a while he and his pilotman went to the signal box, carrying out Rule 55. The signalman explained to them that the train in front was having difficulty in climbing the bank. The shunter in the rear was short of steam; the train engine, an 0-6-0 goods, was also in trouble with steam. Both engines had stopped for a blow-up and considerable delay was being caused on the railway.

To the pilotman's amazement, Gerry suggested to the signalman that he allow him to enter the next block and give both down-and-out engines a push. Gerry said that he came up to the rear of the train, and when he opened her up she did not slip at all. Not only did he push up two engines and 30 wagons, but pulled up his own train as well.

Marsh tells an interesting story about the 'electric' acceleration of the Bulleid pacifics:

In 1952 I was in the No 3 link, the 'Tavy Gang', with driver Harry Pope and we used to have a turn regarded as a light duty for the engine. We would sign on at about 3.00pm and work the 3.54pm with about five to seven bogies on to Basingstoke, stopping at Woking and all stations. On arrival at Basingstoke we used to come off and work a parcels and passenger train to Waterloo, leaving Basingstoke about 6.35pm and arriving at Waterloo just after 8.00pm. On this particular day we had Merchant Navy No 35016 *Elders Fyffes*. A most unusual feature about this particular turn was that, as far as I know, it was the only steam passenger train that ran from Woking to Surbiton on the up local. We left Woking about a minute ahead of the up Portsmouth electric and were due to cross over on to the up main line behind it at Hampton Court Junction. We had been going for a couple of minutes when the up Pompey electric caught us up, and with a couple of toots on the hooter, opened-up, almost leaving us standing.

[With full regulator and 40 percent cut-off, No 35016 went in pursuit.] The up local line was so rough that I could not stand up to fire to her, and indeed she was rolling so much that I had to hang on. It was all right for Harry as he still had hold of the regulator. We began to catch up with the Pompey and then overtook it. At Hampton Court Junction we had to wait several minutes for the electric to pass so that we could carry on behind it. Our arrival at Waterloo was several minutes early, catching the station staff on the hop. A parson came up and said, 'I saw what you did; it was nice to put them in their place', and he gave us 10 shillings – a lot of money in those days.

A few weeks later a friend of mine had this same turn and entered the same race. As the Pompey passed them, the chef leaned out of the dining kitchen and handed them a tray containing silver teapot, sugar, milk jug, cups and saucers; and off went the Pompey. After they had drunk the tea the driver said, 'We had better return the crockery.' They raced after the Pompey, caught it, and knocked on the kitchen window. They said, 'You should have seen the chef's face when he opened the window, to be handed his crocks with thanks.'

Marsh's comments on firing and coal in general are worth recording, as follows:

In the early 1950s at Nine Elms there was a rather controversial fireman named Ron Coffin in the No 2 link and who was in my opinion an excellent fireman. On Bulleids he always ran with about a foot of red-hot fire. On one occasion on the down Atlantic Coast Express he ran into Salisbury with a light fire, as was his custom. The Salisbury fireman was most upset and demanded more fire. Ron stated his willingness to take her through to Exeter with his light fire, but this was refused. In his spare time he used to teach at the Nine Elms Improvement Class and give lectures. I was convinced that he was correct in his theories about firing; indeed he followed the textbook injunctions of 'light bright and tight, with maximum use of dampers and firebox doors to allow primary and secondary air.' In the main, therefore, I used to fire like him.

The type of coal being used made a difference to the manner of firing. When I came out of the army we had Welsh coal, though Tilmanstone coal was used at the Yard. At one time Basingstoke was having Indian coal, and the largest knob I ever saw was the size of a finger nail. It was the worst we ever had. Salisbury had American coal, which was a nice size and gave off a very good heat, but burned very quickly. I remember coming up from Salisbury on a Channel Packet with driver Jerry Sartin, working the 6.33pm to London. We had this American coal and I had the door open two notches. However, the locomotive steaming too well, this coal giving off so much heat that I opened the doors fully and had the fire level with the firehole, getting it completely incandescent. Jerry had not noticed that I had opened the doors wide. He was sitting with his feet on the small wooden block, and suddenly let out a howl, for his trousers were smouldering and his legs burning!

Only the first Bulleid pacifics were being rebuilt when Marsh left the railway service, so that practically all his experience was confined to the unrebuilt engines. When in February 1956 the first of the rebuilds, No 35018 *British India Line* was completed, driver Smaldon and fireman Marsh were among those selected to test the engine, with an inspector travelling on the footplate. A few weeks later it was put on the Bournemouth Belle; Smaldon and Marsh had her on this turn for quite a considerable time. It was the approaching death of steam that drove that steam enthusiast, Fireman Jim Marsh, from the railway service. He says:

I could never live in England and not work on steam engines. I remember quite well one night in 1956. Although in the top link, I had a spare turn and was doing a shunting duty at Waterloo. I was sitting on this tank engine on Westminster Bridge looking at Big Ben. I could hear it strike midnight and could see the light underneath it, showing that the Commons were still sitting. I had been told by inspector Dan Knight that the road to Bournemouth would be electrified before 1970. I did not wish to drive electrics and I was not keen on diesels. I had worked on Nos 10000, 10001, 10201, 10202, and 10203 and was not impressed. A friend of mine had said that steam engines were dying. I did not wish to be there to see the change, so sitting there on Westminster Bridge I realised that my idyllic life was coming to its end. To make a clean break, my wife and

I moved to Jersey, as there was no way that I could have stayed on the mainland and not worked on the railways.

It is easy to understand Marsh's decision. The dedicated steam locomotive man loved his job. It will be apparent from what has been written above, that the driving and firing of the great express passenger engines were arts in which their highest expression could only be obtained by the few who were the really great craftsmen of their trade. It was because this supreme excellence had been reached in their respective spheres by men like Smaldon and Marsh that the push-button predictability of diesels and electrics could make no appeal. Many lesser practitioners in the steam world appreciated the change to the cleaner working conditions and comfortable cabs of the new motive power (though some have expressed later doubts to the author as to the benefit to their health), but it is difficult to believe that there can be the same pride in the job.

The Bulleid pacifics as modified were the last express engines produced for British Railways, and the Merchant Navys in their new guise may have been the best of the top power class; that LMS steam enthusiast, the late Roland Bond, admitted that they might be as good as the Stanier pacifics. Fittingly, they hauled the last regular steam expresses. They were lovely to look at, and during their last weeks of service I would watch them tearing through Winchfield station on the London & South Western main line or coming slowly and majestically into Waterloo. For me that great station is now flat and lifeless, for the soul has gone out of it.

9 Steam Reminiscences of the Bulleid Era

From 1941 until 1957 the unrebuilt Bulleid pacifics dominated Southern express passenger haulage, and as recorded in the previous chapter delighted drivers and firemen alike with their performance. The rebuilding of the engines owed nothing to criticisms by the footplate men, but was inspired solely by the costs of maintaining them and keeping them running. Before discussing the weaknesses in the original design which led to the decision to rebuild, some of Jim Marsh's other stories about the unrebuilt engines are well worth recounting. A background to these, which can hardly be omitted, concerns Marsh's father, for it shows something of the old London & South Western atmosphere.

Marsh senior lived in Crimsworth Road (a short street running parallel to Wandsworth Road) in a house whose back garden overlooked part of the Nine Elms 'A' Yard; both he and his brother – perhaps inevitably – worked on the LSWR. Marsh's father started as a Nine Elms van boy on 5 July 1915. When he was on night duty he was quite often a 'spare' and was used as a 'knocker-up'. This entailed rousing men who were needed for early workings. One morning, at about half past three he was sent to the home of a cartage driver to call him for an immediate task . . . Later that morning, Marsh senior was summoned to the governors' office. It transpired that the driver had come in late and had stated that the knocker-up had not called. The driver's word was accepted and Marsh was given the admonition that if he wished to remain on the South Western he had better mend his ways. One of Marsh's mates told him on the next occasion that he had to call this particular driver to chalk his initials on a wall, which he did. At 10.00am another knocker-up arrived with the message, 'The Guv'nor wants you straight away.' The same three people were in the office and there was the same assurance from the driver that the knocker-up had not called and hence he had been late for duty. When asked for an explanation Marsh played his trump card. 'I can prove I called', he said, 'Because I chalked my initials on the side of his house.' A foreman was summoned to go to the house in company with the driver but on arrival at the driver's home Marsh's face dropped, for there were no initials on the wall! The driver had apparently spotted the initials before going to work and had washed them off. Back at the office Marsh was told he had been proved a liar and that his future on the South Western was very doubtful. In due course Marsh, senior, again on night duty was told to go to the home of this same driver and tell him to come to work immediately. In response to the knock he gave the same reply. The knocker-up called again at 10.00am with a summons to the office. As he entered the driver was saying, 'You know what youngsters are today, Sir; all lazy and you can't trust any of them.' It looked as if Marsh was really in trouble and likely to be sacked, but he produced his ace . . . 'This time I can really prove I knocked him up,' he said, and from under his coat he produced a door knocker. 'I unscrewed this from his front door.' There was a hush: the foreman was summoned again and off went the trio to the driver's house from which the door knocker was indeed missing!

Marsh makes an interesting point about the pride which footplatemen had in the appearance of their locomotives. It was a pride which stemmed from a genuine affection for them – an affection which animated those who designed, built, and maintained them. There is a mystique surrounding this almost human machine which is quite absent from the diesel or electic locomotive. Why this is so it is not easy to explain. The steam locomotive requires considerable skill to drive and fire and it will

West Country class Pacific No 34023 *Blackmore Vale* (nameplate removed) on the Swanage branch after working the special Dorset Coast Express on 7 May 1967. It is now preserved on the Bluebell Railway (*D. H. Ballantyne*)

provide bursts of power beyond its theoretical limits, while the diesel or electric locomotive is entirely predictable and cannot produce more energy than is built into it. Again, artistry in the drawing office can result in a steam locomotive that is a thing of beauty, whereas nothing can make a diesel or electric look other than a box on wheels. Finally, one can see nearly all the 'works' of the steam engine while those of its rivals and successors are hidden. Marsh mentions a photograph which appeared in a railway publication of a cleaner at Feltham who, after cleaning a Maunsell 4-6-0, had drawn in chalk a large white star on the front of the smokebox. The caption to the photograph was, 'A Labour of Love'.

Marsh has an amusing story which shows the lengths to which the best footplatemen would go in beautifying their engines. He writes:

I remember in the summer of 1953 working the Bournemouth Belle with Walter Hooper, a real gentleman and a good driver, a West Countryman who never flapped and gave one much of the confidence he radiated. Signing on at Nine Elms, he had his own green-painted Channel Packet, No 35012 *United States Lines*. It had been prepared for us and we had a really good trip both ways. On arrival at Bournemouth West we turned around the triangle at Branksome and, after our break, went back tender-first to Bournemouth West. On our way to the 'West' we stopped at a signal on one of the bridges. I noted that there were a couple of railway painters painting a bridge. They had a pot of silver anti-rust paint and they were using an unusual type of brush, which was rather like a school paste brush. It had a handle about a foot long, pointed at one end, and with the bristles coming out of the side at the other end.

Although the footplate had been cleaned before leaving London, I had taken a bit out of the fire at Branksome and the boiler front had become a little dusty. In the cab of these locomotives the boiler front was painted a pinky brown. As this was Wally's own engine, the pipes, oil boxes, and brass surrounds were very clean. However, affixed to the cab boiler front were a number of brass identification plates. It was very difficult to clean these because inside the plate they were very rough cast. I decided to spruce up the engine a bit, and when one of the painters turned his back I jumped down off the footplate and 'won' his brush and paint. I painted the identification plates silver and then put a pot of thick vacuum oil all over the boiler front, giving it a really good clean. The identification plates were still painted silver when I left three years later.

The funniest thing about this incident was the look on the painters' faces. They were searching all round for their brush and paint; one of them climbed down the scaffold and looked into the street below, thinking he had dropped it. We set back on our train and passed under the bridge again, where the two painters were still looking for their gear. Walter and I were falling about laughing. I shouted to them, 'Hey, mates, I've got your paint,' but they did not hear above the noise of the engine and train.

The unrebuilt Bulleid Pacifics were capable of very high speeds, though there does not appear to be any official record of the fastest speed attained by any one of them. Rumours there were of phenomenal speeds, but one is reminded of the legendary exploits of Aspinall's Atlantics on the Lancashire & Yorkshire Railway. Marsh recalls an article in a magazine of the early 1950s, called the *Locomotive Express*, in which a driver at Exmouth Junction claimed that with a West Country and ten bogies he had covered 3½ miles in 1½ minutes at an average speed of 140mph! Marsh adds that nobody contradicted this story, and when he showed the article to his driver, Tom Smaldon, the latter said that there were three brothers of this name at Exmouth. He knew them well and the one who wrote the article was not prone to exaggeration. Nevertheless rough timing on an ordinary watch is always suspect; if the time was, say, two minutes, this would bring the speed down to 105mph. Marsh rode on these engines at over 100mph on a number of occasions, and comments that they frequently ran the 26 miles from Worting Junction to Woking in 16½ minutes. He says that. 'The amazing thing about these Bulleid Pacifics was the way they ran.' He goes on:

Tom Smaldon always used a long cut-off of between 20 and 25 percent, and ran on the regulator. I can see him now, sitting on his seat, gently tapping the regulator with his left hand and leaning over slightly towards the firebox, holding out a cloth in his right hand. He kept tapping the regulator until the cloth just wafted in front of the fire. When I had been with him for some time he used to let me drive. I tried this trick with the cloth but always started to lose time. The only conclusion I could come to was that my steam, when I was firing, must have been better than his when he acted as my fireman. He used to laugh at this explanation.

Smaldon would never run early or late, and if for some reason we were behind time he would always make it up. There was however one strange episode. On 27 May 1956 we were booked to work the 6.00pm to Salisbury and signed on at Nine Elms at 4.19pm to prepare our engine, No 34054 *Lord Beaverbrook*. On arrival at our train we had the usual 12 bogies, 400 tons unladen weight. As usual, with most of the Pacifics, the locomotive steamed well. We were on time at Hampton Court Junction and at Woking, but between Woking and Hook our timing suddenly went astray. As we went through Hook station, Tom took out his watch and said, 'My watch has stopped; what's the right time?' I looked at my watch and saw that it registered the same time as his. His watch had not stopped and we had a lot of time in hand. He closed the regulator and free-wheeled to Basingstoke, stopping there in exactly 50 minutes for the 47¾ miles, which was five minutes early. If Smaldon had kept going as he had been, he would have arrived there in from 45 to 47 minutes. He was worried about this early arrival, asking me how it could have occurred: had he worked the engine too hard, or had I been put out? I replied that neither had happened. He had put the cut-off in his usual place, between 20 and 25 percent and had worked the regulator in his usual fashion. It seems that the engine ran so freely that it had swept ahead of Smaldon's calculations.

What could have been happening was that the steam reversing gear was creeping slightly. With worn valve gear the cut-off setting could give a most misleading reading, though heavy spark throwing at the chimney top could warn the driver that he was nearly in full gear.

About two weeks later Marsh had a different experience with a No 2 Link driver, whom he knew well and liked a lot. The turn concerned was a Sunday 6.20pm from Waterloo to Bournemouth, booked to cover the 79 miles to Southampton (where they came off) in 80 minutes. They had the same engine as on the down journey and it behaved beautifully until they were approaching Woking. Here Marsh noticed: 'a sort of buffeting, in which the train appeared to be pushing the engine. This continued through Basingstoke, when we were going really fast. I went over and had a word with my mate, telling him about this feeling. He immediately said, "Oh, I can cure that', and he moved the cut-off to about 20 percent, leaving the regulator alone. The buffeting stopped immediately, and we got a much better ride. Unfortunately he very soon put if back into the middle. Obviously, as the fireman, I could make no further comment, but there was no doubt in my mind that the long cut-off was much the better. It was common knowledge that the steam reverser was notoriously unreliable and I believe that on this journey the driver must have been working almost in

116

reverse. I think that many drivers worked the engines in the middle under the impression that this was economical and saved the fireman work; but in my opinion this often was not so, especially with a Bulleid pacific' As compared with the previous journey, in this one the reverser was probably creeping backwards instead of forwards.

One cannot leave the Bulleid era without mentioning the remarkable Q1 class 0-6-0 goods engines. Their production was due to a request from the operating department in 1941 for more 0-6-0s. Maunsell's Q class 0-6-0s had been built in response to the need to replace the very useful Adams Jubilee class mixed-traffic 0-4-2 engines in the haulage of secondary freight and passenger services. Since greater adhesion was needed a 2-6-0 design was first considered, but because money was short it was decided that a 0-6-0 would do. An order for 20 locomotives was placed with Eastleigh Works. They were designated Class Q, and the last was completed as World War II broke out. They had 19in by 26in cylinders and 5ft 1in wheels. On the services for which Maunsell had designed them they worked well, but unfortunately they were used on heavy main line duties for which they quite unsuited, and there were consequent complaints of inadequate power, poor steaming, and other faults. However, they were very reliable, and when Bulleid altered one of them by fitting his modified Lemaître blastpipe and large diameter chimney in 1940 there was such an improvement that the whole class was similarly treated.

Bullied agreed that more 0-6-0s were necessary and permission was obtained from the Government to build 40 engines. Bulleid wanted a considerable more powerful engine than Maunsell's Q design, and also one that was sufficiently free-running for a wider range of passenger services. A larger boiler would be necessary together with a carefully designed steam circuit, cylinders, and motion. A wide route availability was essential and the weight of the big boiler envisaged raised a problem. The civil engineer agreed reluctantly to a maximum axle load of 18 tons but hoped for something less. Bulleid therefore aimed at 17 tons and planned to save as much weight as possible by the ruthless elimination of everything that was merely decorative or otherwise not essential. Footplate and splashers were omitted, the smokebox was flat-bottomed, the chimney and dome starkly utility. Because of wartime shortages, it was decided to lag the boiler with Idaglass, a home-produced fibreglass product which could not carry a load. This prohibited the normal cladding and lagging bands so that thin steel frame-supported casing plates were mounted independently of the boiler, presenting a slab-sided appearance and resulting in a locomotive that was practically devoid of curves. Much of this treatment came from the design of the much more presentable pacifics. The result was undeniably hideous, but with its large boiler pressed to 230lb/sq in and excellent steam circuit, the type was an immense success. Cylinders and wheels were of the same dimensions as those of the Q class. Bulleid made a mistake on the brake power which was far too low for such a powerful engine when hauling a heavy load of unfitted wagons. There were many critics of the engine's extraordinary appearance. Stanier, when shown a photograph, exclaimed, 'I don't believe it!', and followed this by asking, 'Where's the key?'

Of these Q1 class 0-6-0s, Marsh writes:

They were probably the worst looking engines ever designed, though I rather liked working on them, even though my experience of firing them was rather limited. I liked the spacious footplate, and unlike Mr Bulleid's pacifics they had an excellent outlook. The enclosed cab was comfortable compared with Southern 0-6-0s, and there is no doubt that the engine was a vast improvement on them. Drummond's 700 class, commonly known as 'Black Motors', were very open, and during inclement weather one had to work under storm sheets. This was very uncomfortable and I hated doing it. The Wainwright O1 class engines, sometimes called the 'Flying Bed-steads', were even worse, for they had hardly any cab at all. Whenever I saw a Wainwright 0-6-0 it always reminded me of Will Hay in *The Ghost Train*.

My firing experience of the Q1s took place during 1952 when I was in the Feltham No 4 Link. We would sometimes have a Q1, or a

'Charlie' as they were called after Mr Bulleid's original lettering and numbering. My first trip on a Q1 was with driver Jack de Barr. We arrived at Feltham Yard and were due to work a freight train to Nine Elms via Chertsey. It was a novel experience, seeing at close quarters and getting onto my first 'Charlie'. I then saw how apt was Sir William Stanier's comment, for the line of boiler plugs in the top of the boiler did in fact look like a row of key-holes. At Feltham the locomotive was already prepared with a nice fire. After leaving Feltham Yard and going through the station, I went over to my mate's side and looked back. They were all coming and we then got the tip from the guard.

After we had been going for a few minutes, I opened the firebox doors and slipped a couple of shovels of coal into the firebox. I brushed the floor, turned round and stood up all in one movement, and in doing so did what every other fireman did who ever worked on a Q1 – cracked my head on the lubricator! I thought I was going to pass out, and for a few minutes the air was blue. It was a ridiculous place for a lubricator. Carrying on, with the locomotive steaming well, we had no trouble up Virginia Water bank. We stopped at Surbiton and Wimbledon for a little shunting, and left the remainder of our train in Nine Elms Yard.

On arriving in the depot we were due to dispose of the engine. My mate went to the office, leaving me in the old shed to clean the smokebox, fire and ashpans. As the procedure was, I cleaned the smokebox first, jumping up on to the framing in front of it and opening the door. That in itself was quite a feat on account of the lack of framing. After cleaning the inside, I forgot how little framing there was in front of the smokebox and stepped back. My mate returned a few minutes later to find me still lying in the pit. I had fallen about seven feet straight on to my back. However, I had been very lucky, for apart from being winded I had no other injuries. Later I discovered that Feltham men used a large plank of wood which had been specially made to fit over the buffers and make the frame longer. Presumably because Nine Elms men did not often use these engines, no one appeared to have heard about the planks; when I made enquiries at our stores there was no record of any request having been made for them.

From Marsh's unfortunate experiences, it would appear that the footplatemen had not been consulted in the design of the engines, and that what appears to be non-essential in the drawing office is not necessarily regarded so by drivers and firemen.

Bulleid numbered these engines C1 to C40, while under British Railways they became Nos 33001 to 33040. One seemed to get used to their appearance, and eventually their very ugliness became oddly attractive. I have encountered this experience amongst men who commonly drove and fired them. Some men became very fond of them, and one ex-fireman of my acquaintance drove his car on a round trip of 140 miles to experience the joy of climbing into the cab of the locomotive preserved on the Bluebell Railway. The last time that I saw one of them in British Railways service was in connection with track relaying in the cutting at the end of my Wokingham garden. The engine was dirty, but as demonstrating their affection for the class its crew had chalked the old Bulleid number on the smokebox front.

One slightly disconcerting aspect of the Bulleid 0-6-0s was the sight from the cab of naked coupling rods whirling round, with no running plates to give illusory protection if one broke. However, a broken coupling rod was a rare event on the Southern and most men soon got used to this unusual view.

It is interesting and rather strange that some Southern drivers in the 1950s were still fascinated by Churchward's Great Western Railway Pacific, No 111 *The Great Bear*. Marsh remembers them talking about this locomotive as if it had been scrapped only just prior to World War II. He says: 'I can recall a number of South Western men discussing this very large engine, and of some of them asserting that she had very wide firebars so that she would only need to go into the locomotive for fire cleaning once a week, thus saving a great deal of time and money.' Marsh never believed this extraordinary theory because he could recall getting on to Great Western engines at Basingstoke and Salisbury and seeing 'boxes of clinkers up to the firebox doors, and they were never on the road for a week.'

(*previous page*) Bulleid Battle of Britain 4-6-2 No 34054 *Lord Beaverbrook* leaves Exeter St Davids with a Sunday train to Ilfracombe on 3 May 1964 (*D. H. Ballantyne*)

10 The Bulleid/Bond Pacifics

At their best there is not doubt that the performance of the Bulleid Pacifics, whether Merchant Navy of West Country could equal that of any other British express locomotives of their power class. But there were penalties. In 1951 and 1952 tests were conducted at Rugby and on the road between Carlisle and Skipton with Merchant Navy No 35022 *Holland Amerika Line* and a Riddles Britannia class pacific. The boiler efficiency of the two engines was about equal, but the Britannia scored fairly heavily on cylinder efficiency, due it was considered to the faulty distribution of the steam by the Bulleid chain-driven valve gear. In coal consumption the figures for the Merchant Navy were generally quite a lot higher than those for the Britannia, the West Country class locomotives in the 1948 Interchange Trials had a particularly high coal consumption due to the absence of damper doors to the ashpan. The Merchant Navy's water consumption between Carlisle and Skipton was from 4.1% to 16.7% higher than that of the Britannia. The motion of the Bulleid pacific was designed to work in an oil bath, but in practice it was found impossible to make this oil-tight. The leakage was such that in a typical period of 18 months the average consumption of high-quality lubricating oil was just over 31 pints per 100 miles for a Merchant Navy, compared with 9.5 pints for a Lord Nelson.

As already stated, the principal features which had made the Bulleid pacifics unreliable in certain respects were the chain-driven valve gear, the rigidly mounted oil bath, the air-smoothed

Rebuilt West Country class Pacifics No 34016 *Bodmin*, now preserved on the Mid-Hants Railway, and No 34071 *601 Squadron* at Waterloo in the last years of steam working (*K. Field*)

casing, and the steam reversing gear. Valve gear failure was not uncommon, and it was generally due to fracture of the rocker shafts or driving chains or to damage to the valves caused by over-travel. The oil bath, apart from the constant need to top it up, made maintenance more difficult because the big-end and valve gear parts could not be readily examined. In addition, it was very hard to exclude water, so that corrosion appeared in the motion parts. The air-smoothed casing led to fires, which were practically unknown on the more orthodox locomotives, but which in 1953 occurred on 38 Bulleid Pacifics. Most of the fires began near the ashpan hopper doors and were due to the accumulation of oil-soaked inflammable matter; from there they often spread to the boiler lagging plates and clothing. The shape of the casing tended to trap heat from the locomotive and set up temperatures which were about the flashpoint of oil. Once a fire started it spread rapidly under the casing, forming a furnace.

Apart from the fire hazard, the casing was difficult to maintain, and it often hid parts needing attention, so that bits of it had to be taken off to get at them. The steam reversing gear habitually crept away from the position in which it had been set.

In the works considerably more man-hours were required for intermediate and general repairs to the two classes of Bulleid pacifics than for any other British locomotives of comparable size and power. Before his retirement from British Railways R. A. Riddles issued instructions for the locomotives to be rebuilt in order to eliminate the troublesome features of their design. Proposals formulated to implement these instructions envisaged the retention of the boiler, frames, outside cylinders, wheels, axleboxes, and the removal or replacement of the chain-driven valve gear with its rocker shafts, the inside cylinder, the smokebox, the superheater header, the steam pipes etc, the reversing gear, the piston heads and rods, the oil bath, the air-smoothed casing, the mechanical lubricators, the regulator, the ashpan and grate, the cylinder cocks, and the sandboxes. It will be observed that all these measures were improvements to an otherwise excellent design. Their purpose was to provide a locomotive with three independent sets of Walschaert valve gear, a screw reversing gear, a circular smokebox fixed to a saddle for more robust construction, normal type of boiler clothing, and footplating along the sides of the engine.

The late Roland Bond told me much about the Bulleid Pacifics and his opinions are well summarised in his own book. Although as chief mechanical engineer British Railways, Bond presided over the initial stages of the supersession of steam by diesel traction, he was to the end of this life one of the greatest steam locomotive enthusiasts that I have met. Of the Merchant Navy and West Country Pacifics he wrote:

These remarkable locomotives won for themselves an assured place in the history of British locomotive engineering by their performance with the fastest and heaviest expresses on the Southern system. But they were expensive to operate and maintain. They acquired a reputation entirely consistent with that of their designer. Seldom

125

content with the conventional, however well proved in service, Bulleid introduced many novel features in these engines, intended to reduce the extent and cost of maintenance. But they had the opposite effect to that intended, and were moreover the direct cause of their coal and water – to say nothing of lubricating oil – consumption being significantly higher than that of other contemporary locomotives of comparable power. The notorious chain-driven valve gear, buried inaccessibly in its oil bath, was the main cause of the unreliablility, failures in service, and loss of availability from which these engines suffered. Steam distribution was very erratic, leading to low cylinder efficiency, and coal and water consumption about 15 percent higher than that of most other modern locomotives.

The so-called air-smoothed boiler casing was the cause of much trouble and expense in maintenance. It contributed directly to the unique propensity of these engines to catch fire! Oil vapour and leakage from the oil bath tended to saturate the boiler lagging; and it only required some hot cinders from the ashpan hopper doors to start a conflagration which sometimes required the attention of the local fire brigade. Minor modifications had done little to eliminate the troublesome features of these engines. There was a clear case for major rebuilding, drawings for which were prepared at Brighton in close collaboration with my staff at Marylebone. The reliability of the rebuilt locomotives was improved as much as their external appearance. Coal and water consumption in everyday service were reduced by about 10 percent. A day out on the footplate on one of the rebuilt Merchant Navys working the Bournemouth Belle confirmed to my satisfaction that the rebuilding was a thoroughly sound job.

I told Bond when we were discussing the rebuilding that as chief mechanical engineer at the time he had every right to be given the credit for the revision which had produced the last British Railways steam locomotive design. He agreed, but he was a very modest man and preferred that such recognition should be initiated by somebody else. This, somewhat belatedly, I am trying to do.

It was proposed that the 30 Merchant Navy class engines should be modified first, followed by the 110 West Country class. Approval for the conversion of the Bulleid pacifics was given, but initially for only 30 of either class during 1955 and 1956. The reason for this limitation was the intention by British Railways to

Rebuilt West Country Pacific No 34018 *Axminster* with an express train at Salisbury in 1964 (*John K. Morton*)

change its motive power from steam to diesel or electric. Recommendations for the rebuilding of the remaining locomotives were to be submitted from year to year.

Before the first Merchant Navy had been modified there was a serious failure with No 35016 *Elders Fyffes* on 16 November 1955 at Gillingham, Dorset, when all four coupling rods broke at speed and the bronze driving axleboxes were badly cracked, one of them being completely broken. As there had been previous trouble with the coupling rods it was apparent that they would have to redesigned, and it was decided also to replace the expensive bronze axleboxes with cast-steel ones. These two modifications were added to the list given above.

R. G. Jarvis, Chief Technical Adviser (Locomotives) SR, was responsible for the detailed plans prepared at Brighton for the rebuilding of the locomotives. Jarvis wrote: 'We had to give a good deal of thought to the most economical way of eliminating the troublesome features while retaining other features, such as the boiler and chassis, which were in most respects excellent. The basic scheme was to dispense with the chain-driven valve gear and oil bath, and the air-smooth casing. We used BR standard parts whenever possible, but did not replace any more than was strictly necessary to effect the desired improvements in performance and reliability.'

An interesting aspect of the design lay in having three independent sets of Walschaert valve gear, all driving on the second pair of coupled wheels. It was the alleged impracticability of doing this which has been stated as the main reason for Gresley's derived motion for the inside cylinder. However, Jarvis points out that there had been a successful precedent in Stanier's 3-cylinder tank engines for the Tilbury section of the LMS. Jarvis's letter concludes: 'Certainly the rebuilt Pacifics behaved very well, and Sam Ell, who conducted the test of No 35020, told me that they were the most predictable engines he had ever tested (praise indeed from Swindon).'

I have already mentioned the resemblance of the rebuilt locomotives to a Riddles Britannia class pacific, and this visible inclusion into the BR family likeness had been insisted on by Roland Bond.

The first rebuild, No 35018 *British India Line*, left the erecting shop at Eastleigh on 9 February 1956. Of its arrival at Nine Elms and subsequent history, Marsh writes:

In April 1956 the first rebuilt Channel Packet arrived. It was No 35018 *British India Line*. Prior to being rebuilt she had always been an excellent machine. In the middle of April 1956 I was in the top link with Tom Smaldon, and every other day we were on the Bournemouth Belle and were booked the rebuilt 35018. We started work at 11.20am in the shed, and as was the custom she was prepared and on the pit waiting for us. On arrival at Waterloo we picked up inspector Bert Plummer, a travelling footplate inspector who was to ride with us to see how the locomotive would perform. He carried a clipboard with a schedule on it, which included mileposts, stations,

Rebuilt Merchant Navy class Pacific No 35008 *Orient Line* returning to Waterloo with a BR special commemorating the last day of Southern steam on 2 July 1967 (*John Goss*)

and timings. We had a glorious trip down. Other than when stopping at Southampton and Bournemouth, she stayed glued between 240 and 250lb/sq in, but she never blew off at the valves once. On dropping our train at Bournemouth West we went into Branksome to prepare for the return. On the way up she again behaved impeccably, the pressure remaining at 240/250lb/sq in and the water just bobbing in the top nut; Bert still scribbled out his schedule and counted the shovels of coal. As always with Tom Smaldon we were on time at Waterloo for as he dropped the handle the big hand on the station clock moved to 6.50pm. I fired to No 35018 many more times between then and resigning at the end of June.

No doubt there will always be controversy as to which was the better engine – the original or the rebuild. I always regarded the original as the finest engine in Britain, if only a screw reverser could have been fitted and the smoke and exhaust steam hanging down one side could have been cured. I felt that No 35018 as rebuilt should have behaved well because she was virtually a new engine and an Eastleigh one at that. I can well remember when a few months previously I saw No 30752 *Linette* on the down Royal Wessex with 13 bogies – usually this train merited a West Country. I spoke to the fireman who said that she had only been out of Eastleigh shops a couple of weeks. Both he and the driver stated that No 30752 in her then condition could have timed any train in Britain, including 'even your Belle', which then had 12 Pullmans and a van, with an unladen weight of 515 tons. The Urie Arthurs were never as good as the Scotsmen, which showed that when Eastleigh serviced an engine they certainly made a good job of it.

It was perhaps fitting that towards the end of steam one of the last class of London & South Western express locomotives should be displaying such marked ability.

There will no doubt be arguments about the relative merits of the original and rebuilt Pacifics as long as men remember steam on the lines of the old London & South Western. But whatever marginal differences there may have been in performance on the road, the rebuilds were infinitely superior in consistency of performance, particularly after high mileages, and their vastly reduced maintenance requirements were an inestimable boon at a time when the recruitment of running shed fitters was particularly difficult. Maintenance costs were reduced as well, and there were further savings in the much less time taken in disposal work. This saving was primarily due to rocking grates that really worked, so that a rebuilt engine could be disposed within an hour, as compared with the two hours normally required with an unmodified pacific, owing to the lengthy business of cleaning fires with the clinker shovel through the firehole door.

The rebuilt engines included many improvements for the enginemen. The lookout in both directions was improved and the fully wrapped boiler with smoke deflectors eliminated the trouble experienced with smoke and steam obscuring the vision. In addition, the cabs were not so hot in summer, the sanding gear worked properly, an improved regulator controlled much of the slipping, the cut-off setting was locked and could not creep, and the water gauges could be read by both driver and fireman without leaving their seats.

Nevertheless, the solid virtues of these reformed ladies of the road failed to seduce the affections of many of the enginemen who had fallen under the spell of Bulleid's mercurial maidens!

11 Royal Derby

The first race trains in the world were run by the London & South Western Railway, and since those early days the line between Waterloo and Clapham Junction has probably handled more race traffic than any other section of railway.

An account of these first trains for a race meeting is given by W. M. Ackworth in his book *The Railways of England*. He writes:

> But difficulties of quite another kind fell at times to the lot of the South Western. One of its earliest experiences was of the 'Derby' that occured a week after the opening of the line, in the last days of May 1838. The Company had advertised their intention of running eight trains to Kingston, and to their astonishment early in the morning a crowd of 5,000 persons assembled at Nine Elms. Several trains were despatched, but the crowd increased faster than the trains could carry them off, and at length the mob broke the doors from their hinges, and forcing their way into the station took possession of a 'special' that had been chartered by a private party. In the end the police had to be sent for, and at twelve o'clock a notice in the booking office window announced that no more trains would be run that day.

The Times of 29 May 1838 carried an advertisement in connection with the above saying that extra trains for the Epsom races would be run on the Tuesday, Wednesday, Thursday and Friday of that week to a point on the railway south of Kingston which was nearest to Epsom. The result of this advertisement was narrated as follows in *The Times* of 31 May:

> It is speaking very much within bounds to say that at an early hour upwards of 5,000 persons were assembled at the gates of the

Bulleid West Country class 4-6-2 No 34011 *Tavistock* passing Chessington with the Royal train on Derby Day, 2 June 1954, with Fireman Jim Marsh on the footplate (Courtesy *J. Marsh*)

Southampton Railway at Nine Elms near Vauxhall, for the purpose of going by the railroad trains to the Kingston station and from thence by other conveyances to the race course. The steamboats which ply from London Bridge and from Hungerford were filled with passengers who made sure of getting down to Epsom by the railroad. Hundreds were fated to be disappointed. There were ten times more applicants for seats in the train vans than there were seats for their accommodation. The proprietors did what they could to meet the demands for conveyance but they could not do what was impossible.

It was not recorded what engines hauled these trains, but the company's stock of engines in May 1938 consisted of four 2-2-2s built by C. Tayleur and two by G & J Rennie. They must all have been pressed into service. The above is just a preliminary to fireman Jim Marsh's great day, for he regarded Derby Day, 2 June 1954 as perhaps the proudest moment of his railway life. He was selected to be fireman on West Country No 34011 *Tavistock*, which was to head the Royal Train from Chessington to

ROYAL TRAIN – DERBY DAY 2 JUNE 1954

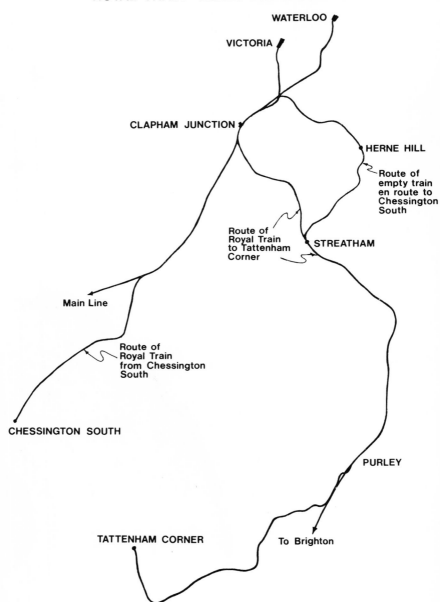

Waterloo. *Tavistock* had been stopped for three days before the event, during which it had been highly polished and its rods so burnished that they shone like silver. Marsh says: 'We had chief travelling inspector Dan Knight on the footplate. He took the four headcode boards out of a special box and would not let me handle them in case I got them dirty. They had a small gold handle on top and a gold band round the edges. A member of the public took a photograph of the train on its way to Waterloo, and sent it to me. I had a painting done from this photograph in 1959 and it now hangs in my home.'

The movements of the Queen were by train from Victoria to Tattenham Corner on the Wednesday, Derby Day, after the races, by car to Chessington South station, and thence by train to Waterloo. The following Friday she travelled again by train to Tattenham Corner to see the Oaks, but she did not return to London after the day's racing. A special operating notice was issued in connection with the Royal Train movement, which read as follows:

Notice of Royal Train Victoria to Tattenham Corner Wednesday 2nd and Friday 4th June, and Chessington South to Waterloo Wednesday 2nd June 1954. This Notice must be acknowledged immediately by use of the enclosed form. The instructions contained in Railway Executive Circular O/RR, dated December 1950, under the heading 'Instructions to be observed in connection with the working of trains designated by the code word *Grove*' and subsequent amendments thereto, must be applied to the train in this notice which is marked *Grove*. [Detailed timings followed].
Formation of 12.10pm Victoria to Tattenham Corner (Wednesday and Friday)
Engine: No 30936 (Schools Class)
Pullman cars (gangways connected):
Isle of Thanet (brake leading) – for servants
Aries (kitchen leading) – for Royal Household
Hercules – For HM The Queen
Minerva (brake trailing) – for railway officers
[The return from Chessington South at 5.15pm was in converse order]

Rebuilt West Country class Pacific No 34022 *Exmoor* at Waterloo (*Kenneth Field*)

SPECIAL WORKING INSTRUCTIONS

Tattenham Corner – Dock Siding

The Dock Siding alongside No 6 platform at Tattenham Corner must be cleared of all vehicles and possession given to the Engineer's Department at 10.00am on Wednesday 2nd June for the erection of temporary bridges spanning the Dock Siding.

Points No 36 must be clipped and padlocked to prevent any vehicle or engine being let into the Dock Siding whilst these bridges are in position.

The Engineer's Department will remove the bridges and give up possession of the Dock Siding at approximately 3.00pm on Friday 4th June.

Stopping Point. At Tattenham Corner the *Grove* train must be brought to a stand with the centre of the engine footplate opposite to a point indicated by a distinctive white mark on the platform at which a Handsignalman with a red hand signal will be stationed to indicate the place at which the train must stop. Another man will be stationed in the six-foot way opposite the white mark for a similar purpose. The distance from the centre of the engine footplate to the centre of the leading doorway of Pullman Car *Hercules* from which Her Majesty will alight at Tattenham Corner is as follows: 157 feet 2½ inches

Stopping Point. At Waterloo the *Grove* train must be brought to a stand with the centre of the engine footplate opposite to a point indicated by a distinctive white mark on the platform at which a Handsignalman with a red hand signal will be stationed to indicate the place at which the train must stop. Another man will be stationed in the six-foot way opposite the white mark for a similar purpose. The distance from the centre of the engine footplate to the centre of the rear doorway of Pullman Car "Hercules" from which Her Majesty will alight at Waterloo is as follows: 150 feet 5¾ inches

Working of Automatic Brake
At Victoria and at Chessington South when the train engine has been coupled to the train and the automatic brake tested by the Guard, the Driver to re-create the vacuum and apply the hand brake on the engine which must remain on until the signal to start is given.

Special Opening of Signal Boxes. The following Signal Boxes to be specially opened for the passage of the *Grove* train and must remain open until the Train out of Section has been received for the special train:

Thornton Heath (Wednesday and Friday), Tolworth (Wednesday), Earlsfield (Wednesday)

Train Reporting. The time at which the *Grove* train has left, passed or arrived, must be reported from the following stations to the District Officer, who in turn must take steps to see that information is passed forward to Headquarters immediately after receipt of each message:

Victoria, East Croydon, Purley, Tattenham Corner, Chessington South, Raynes Park, Clapham Junction and Waterloo.

Enginemen and Guards of the Grove Trains

12.10pm Victoria	5.15pm Chessington South
(Wednesday and Friday)	*(Wednesday)*
Driver, G. King	Driver, W. R. Rose
Fireman, W. Reynolds	Fireman, J. W. Marsh
Guard, A. Bryant	Guard, A. Bryant

Inspector. Inspector Gaylard will travel with the *Grove* trains and must enter in his report the number of persons (other than railway officers) who travel in the Royal trains.

Standby Engines. Standby engines to be provided as follows:–

Victoria	From 11.20am until 12.30pm (Wednesday and Friday)
East Croydon `	From 10.40am until 1.15pm (Wednesday and Friday)
Purley	From 12.0 noon until 1.15pm (Wednesday and Friday)
Chipstead (Down side)	From 12.0 noon until 1.15 p.m. (Wednesday and Friday)
Raynes Park Goods Yard	4.30pm until 5.45pm (Wednesday)
Chessington South	From 4.30pm until 6.00pm (Wednesday)

The train movements involved are of considerable interest. The first of these was that of the empty train from Stewarts Lane Depot to Victoria, arriving there at 11.07am. No 30936 *Cranleigh* then backed on. At 12.10pm the train left Victoria and arrived at Tattenham Corner at 12.54pm. The empty train departed from Tattenham Corner at 2.30pm, still behind *Cranleigh*, reaching Streatham at 3.14pm. There *Cranleigh* came off and was replaced by an engine which left Stewarts Lane motive power depot at 2.08pm, arriving at Streatham at 2.42pm. It departed from Streatham with the empty train at 3.19pm and ran to Chessington South where it arrived at 4.04pm. Meanwhile No 34011 *Tavistock* left Nine Elms Motive Power Depot at 3.49pm, running light to Chessington South, arriving there at 4.23pm.

The Queen, having left the Epsom racecourse by road, boarded the train at Chessington South. Departing at 5.15pm, the Royal Train steamed into Waterloo at 5.40pm. At 6.00pm the empty train left Waterloo behind another engine for Stewarts

Lane, where it arrived at 7.40pm. On Friday 4 June the Royal Train returned to Victoria at the same timings as on the Wednesday, and ran at the same timings to Tattenham Corner. The empty train returned from Tattenham Corner at 2.20pm, but this time ran straight to Stewarts Lane as the Queen did not return to London.

Other points of particular interest are the amount of detailed arrangements which had to be made, the meticulous timings of the train to half minutes, and the stopping point at Waterloo, worked out to 5¾ inches; for 6 inches was not accurate enough!

Index